the
soapmaker

the
soapmaker

natural handmade soap from your kitchen

Janita Morris

Watson-Guptill Publications
New York

For the magnificent seven:

**Nanny and Gaga, mom and Frank, Uncle David, my husband David,
and my beautiful daughter Jemina.**

First published in the United States in 2000 by
Watson-Guptill Publications
770 Broadway
New York, NY 10003
www.watsonguptill.com

Library of Congress Card Number: 00-103121

ISBN 0-8230-4866-7

This book was designed and produced by
Collins & Brown Ltd
London House
Great Eastern Wharf
Parkgate Road
London SW11 4NQ

Editorial Director: Sarah Hoggett
Editors: Clare Stewart and Katie Hardwicke
Designer and Stylist: Alison Lee, Creative Bubble
Photographer: Siân Irvine

The publishers have made every effort to insure that all the instructions given in
this book are accurate and safe, but they cannot accept liability, whether direct or
consequential and however arising. If you are pregnant or have any known or suspected
allergies—or are acutely sensitive to particular plants, oils, dyes, herbs, spices, or other
substances—you may want to consult a doctor about possible adverse reactions
before undertaking the projects in this book. Techniques and materials in
this book are not for children.

Manufactured in Hong Kong

2 3 4 5 6 / 05 04 03 02

contents

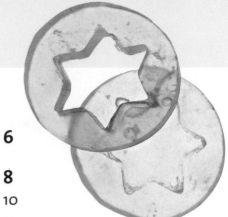

introduction

The notion of soap and cleansing as ritual and enticement has been with us for over three thousand years. The word "soap" derives from the Roman legend of Mount Sapo, which recounts how animals were sacrificed on the top of the mountain. The rain then washed a mixture of wood ash and melted animal fats into the Tiber river below and the amalgam – a soapy substance – proved useful in cleaning clothing and skin.

The first known written mention of soap refers to its use for washing wool, and dates from about 2500 BC. The Ebers Papyrus, a medical document dating from 1500 BC, shows that Egyptians combined animal and vegetable oils with alkaline salts to create a substance similar to soap for washing. One of the first soap factories was discovered in the 1860s when the historic city of Pompeii in southern Italy, buried under lava in AD 79, was excavated.

After the fall of the Roman Empire in AD 467, the interest in bathing declined, and was not revived until several centuries later. During the seventh century, soapmakers' guilds began to spring up in Europe. Early production centers for soap were established in France, Italy, and Spain, and soap soon became a luxury item, heavily taxed and available only to the rich.

Home production of soap was an essential part of the seasonal cycle for the new settlers in America, and it was not until the eighteenth century that commercial soapmaking began. In the mid-nineteenth century, the soap company Pears produced a transparent soap using "the flowers of an English garden" and mass production of scented soap began.

The pleasures of bathing today have sadly been clouded by the use of synthetic scents in soapmaking. Soap and perfumery have long been associated with each other, and with this in mind, I set out to show how soapmaking at the kitchen table can be fun, easy, and aromatic. As a natural perfumer, I find that combining essences from the plant, rather than using synthetic versions, is extremely enriching and enjoyable. The scent is quite different – fresher and true to the natural plant or flower, often with a stronger intensity. When starting to develop the recipes in this book, I knew that I didn't want to use caustic soda (lye), nor make up bubble baths, liquid soaps, or shampoos from scratch. By purchasing fine-quality essential oils and absolutes, along with natural base products, I was able to create recipes that are natural, fragrant, gentle, and easy to follow.

By following any of these recipes you will have produced an item at the end of a couple of hours that is good enough to present as a gift and also have a real sense of making something that is aromatically satisfying.

I hope that within these pages you will find something to inspire you.

Janita Morris

getting started

utensils

All the equipment required for natural soapmaking can be found in a well-equipped kitchen. A double boiler is very useful but you can also use a saucepan with a heatproof bowl as an alternative. A food processor is ideal for grinding the soap flakes for use in the soap balls, but a mortar and pestle will also achieve good results.

There is a never-ending source of molds. Rectangular plastic containers are ideal as they flex when turning out the set soap blocks, but you can use shaped molds or cookie cutters to achieve different effects.

If you want to make something more exotic looking, there are some marvelous flexible plastic molds that are used for plaster casting and are perfect for molding glycerin soaps. The plaster cast molds come in a variety of different shapes, sizes, and themes – such as stars, hearts, and flowers – and can usually be found in arts and craft shops or from the suppliers listed on pages 124–125.

Always wash your soapmaking equipment thoroughly after use, and keep your utensils separately from cooking equipment. Do not use your soapmaking utensils for cooking purposes.

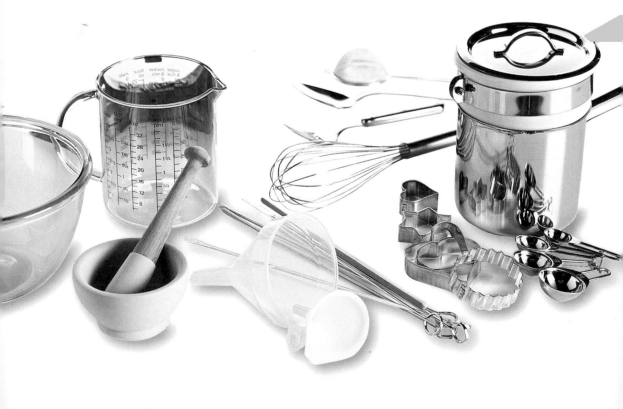

UTENSILS LIST

cookie cutters — For cutting shaped soap.

double boiler — For melting soap flakes or pellets.

electric beater — An electric beater or hand whisk makes light work of the whipped cream soaps.

glass mixing bowl — Choose a size that will accommodate all the ingredients. Very useful for the soap ball recipes.

glass pipette or dropper — For adding drops of base color or essential oils.

hand grater — For grating glycerin blocks.

heatproof measuring cup — For measuring liquids and heating in a microwave.

measuring spoons — These can be plastic or metal.

metal fork/spoon — For mixing dry ingredients. A spoon is also useful for smoothing the surface of melted soap.

mortar and pestle — For grinding soap flakes or spices.

paper towels — For greasing molds.

plastic molds — A range of sizes will give you a variety of soaps. A standard rectangular mold, $5 \times 6\frac{1}{2} \times 2\frac{1}{2}$ in ($13 \times 16.5 \times 6.6$ cm) has been used in the recipes.

sharp knife and ruler — For trimming and cutting blocks of soap.

skewers or chopsticks — For stirring melting soap.

waxed paper — Allows the soaps to dry uniformly.

ingredients

Soapmaking need not be expensive. There are plenty of natural ingredients that can be found in your kitchen cupboards or garden – spices for color, dried herbs or flowers for texture, vegetable and sunflower oils for blending. The base soap ingredients, such as soap flakes or glycerin blocks and pellets, can be readily obtained from the suppliers listed on pages 124–125.

basic soapmaking kit

You will need soap flakes for making whipped cream soaps or soap balls, and glycerin pellets or block glycerin for glycerin soaps. Soap flakes are hand-milled soap that has been grated into fine flakes. You can grind them further for use in soap balls or melt for whipped cream soaps. Glycerin soap pellets melt easily to give a transparent soap. You can also grate blocks of unperfumed cream or glycerin soaps to use as base ingredients.

Include a few essential oils. I suggest starting with a single note, such as citrus. The citrus oils are relatively inexpensive and, hence, cost effective when you start out. You will also need sunflower oil and bottled water for whipped cream soaps.

To add natural color to your soap, follow the simple recipes on page 17, based on readily available spices and essential oils.

base ingredients

I have extended the recipes in this book to include liquid soaps, shower gels, and bubble baths, together with other bath products such as body lotions, shampoos, and conditioners. The bases for these recipes are available readymade from the suppliers listed on pages 124–125. They are white creams or liquids and are fragrance-free, ready for customizing with scented blends and natural colors.

essential oils and absolutes

Essential oils are available in 10 ml (⅓ oz) bottles, sufficient for several batches of soap. Although absolutes are more expensive (they are more concentrated than essential oils), you can buy them in smaller quantities.

Some oils are best avoided if you have highly sensitive skin, suffer from asthma or allergies, or are pregnant. Please see cautions in the aroma profiles, pages 18–20.

shelf life

Give yourself a "best before" date of 18 months after making your recipe.

Occasionally, a brown liquid may appear on the top of your liquid preparations, such as lotions or liquid soaps. These are the vegetable, essential, absolute, or herbal oils separating. Simply shake well before using.

Additional Ingredients

Some of the recipes call for more unusual ingredients than those found in a kitchen cupboard. Many of these can be purchased from food or health stores, or can be obtained from the specialist suppliers listed on pages 124–125.

arrowroot – a white powder. A good thickener for creams and acts as an absorbent in body powders. Available from food and health stores.

beeswax pellets – the bleached, white variety is recommended for cosmetic use. A traditional ingredient of cosmetic preparations, it helps to firm creams and ointments. Available from health stores and specialist suppliers.

bicarbonate of soda (baking soda) – a white powder. Useful dissolved in bath water to alleviate irritated skin. Available from food stores.

citric acid – white powder, derived from the fermentation of sugars from citrus fruits. Has antioxidant and preservative properties. Available from drug stores.

cocoa butter – supplied as a pale yellow-colored block. Good for softening and protecting dry skin. Available from specialist suppliers.

dispersa (surfactant) – a yellow, syrupy liquid. Enables essential oils and water to mix together, creating an opaque looking liquid that is light and refreshing on the skin. Available from specialist suppliers.

dried flowers – dried flower petals, such as lavender and marigold. Add color and texture to soaps. Available from health stores or specialist suppliers.

green clay – a dried powder with a light green color. Useful for tissue repair, drawing out toxins, and calming inflammation. Available from specialist suppliers.

hydrolats (flower waters) – clear or lightly colored scented water. A by-product of the steam distillation of a plant, such as rose, orange flower, lavender, and neroli. Good for toning and freshening the skin. Available from health stores and specialist suppliers.

laundry starch – a white powder that is used to combine ingredients. Available from general stores and specialist suppliers.

liquid glycerin (glycerol/glycerine) – a syrupy, clear liquid. Good for moisturizing sore skin. Available from specialist suppliers.

macerated oils – liquid oils produced by macerating plant material in a fixed oil (usually vegetable oil) which gives the oil the active constituents of the plant and its benefits. They can be incorporated into creams or scent blends. Examples include calendula, passion flower, and St John's Wort. Available from specialist suppliers.

monoi de Tahiti – a white, soft block. Becomes viscous when melted and added to soap recipes to impart the scent of monoi de Tahiti (gardenia flowers). Available from specialist suppliers.

monoi soap pellets – brown pellets scented with gardenia that can be used to make soaps either on their own or combined with base soap flakes. Available from specialist suppliers.

oat plant milk – a white-colored liquid made with natural lipids, vegetable proteins, or sugars. Very soft and mild, ideal as a hair and skin conditioner and can be added to shampoos and bubble baths. Has softening and moisturizing properties. Available from specialist suppliers.

orris root powder – a pale yellow powder with a delicate fragrance of violets, derived from the root of the Florentine iris. Used as a fixative for perfumes. Available from health stores and specialist suppliers.

rosehip granules – coarse textured, speckled pink/peach granules that add color and texture to recipes. Available from health stores and specialist suppliers.

rosehip oil – clear liquid. Believed to help with skin regeneration and repair of damaged tissue. Good in facial oils and creams. Available from specialist suppliers.

shea butter (karite nut butter) – supplied as a white-colored, soft block. Protects the skin and promotes skin healing and elasticity. Good for moisturizing dry, damaged, and irritated skin. Available from specialist suppliers.

sweet almond oil – clear liquid. An all-purpose emollient suitable for most skin types. Can be added to lotions and creams. Other nut oils include hazelnut and kukui nut. Available from health and drug stores.

white clay – a dried white powder. Very gentle and suitable for all skin types. Available from specialist suppliers.

wood betony – a dried herb, speckled green in color. Adds texture and color to soaps. Available from health stores and specialist suppliers.

basic techniques

making whipped cream soaps

1½ cups/110g soap flakes • 10 tbsp/150 ml bottled water • 1 tbsp/15 ml glycerin • 1 tbsp/15 ml sunflower oil (optional – gives a lighter soap)

Fill the bottom part of a double boiler halfway with water and place on the stove to heat to a simmer. Put the soap flakes and water in the top pan and add the glycerin and sunflower oil. Stir with a chopstick or skewer. Grease your mold using a paper towel dipped in sunflower oil.

When the mixture is a lumpy paste, remove from the heat and add any essential oil. Whisk by hand or with an electric beater, starting on the lowest setting. Quickly bring up the speed to the highest setting. The soap will begin to look creamy and frothy when it is ready.

Use a metal spoon to transfer the mixture to the greased molds. Smooth the soap with the back of the spoon (dipped in hot water for a smoother finish). Leave in a cool place to set.

making glycerin soaps

2¾ cups/400 g grated block glycerin or glycerin soap pellets

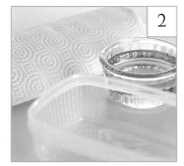

Place the grated glycerin or soap pellets in a double boiler over simmering water to melt. Once the mixture has melted, remove from the heat and add any essential oils.

Grease your mold using a paper towel dipped in a little sunflower oil.

Stir the melted pellets with a spoon or chopstick, then pour the melted mixture into the prepared mold. Leave in a cool place to set for a couple of hours.

making soap balls (no-cook recipe)

3 cups/225 g soap flakes • 1¹/₂ tsp/7.5 ml laundry starch •
5 tbsp/75 ml bottled water

Grind the soap flakes to a gritty powder in a food processor or with a mortar and pestle.

Place the ground soap flakes in a mixing bowl with the laundry starch. Add any color and stir with a fork. Heat the water until hot, either in a microwave or a saucepan. Pour the water into the dry mixture and mix with a fork or spoon.

Knead the mixture until it resembles pastry. Then divide into three sections, each the size of a small apple. Apply a little sunflower oil to clean hands and roll each section into a ball in your hands, smoothing out any irregularities.

cutting soap blocks

Plastic molds will yield a large block of soap that can be divided into smaller sizes.

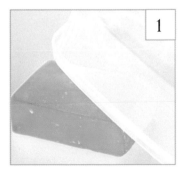

Once the soap has set, turn it out of the plastic mold on to a clean surface.

Use a sharp knife to neaten the edges of the soap. Save any slivers of soap to reuse in another recipe.

Measure the block of soap into equal pieces, either rectangular or square, and cut through with the knife. Alternatively, use a cookie cutter to press out a shape from the soap block.

natural colors

There are many ways to achieve color in your soaps. I have used herbs, spices, and roots mixed with vegetable oil to create a range of base colors with soft, natural shades that cannot be duplicated by chemical dyes. Alternatively, you can use food colorings or wax crayons. Many essential oils have their own color and when added in a blend, especially to the opaque soaps, produce a gentle shade. However, always bear in mind that some oils, such as blue/German chamomile and blue cypress, have their own aroma that may dominate a blend.

People with sensitive skins should avoid using blue/German chamomile essential oil to color their soaps. Use the "green" recipe (opposite) or substitute food colorings or wax crayons.

basic method

Place the chosen colorant and vegetable oil into a microwavable container. Heat in the microwave for one to two minutes on high or place in a saucepan and heat on the stove for three to five minutes. Allow to cool and then strain through a coffee filter or tea strainer into a heatproof bowl. Carefully pour the colored liquid into a glass bottle or jar with a cap and label. The natural coloring is now ready to use as required.

COLOR	INGREDIENTS	METHOD
orange	2 tsp/10 ml paprika 1 tsp/5 ml turmeric 4 tbsp/60 ml vegetable oil	See basic method opposite.
mandarin orange	2 tsp/10 ml mace powder 4 tbsp/60 ml vegetable oil	See basic method opposite.
yellow	2 tsp/10 ml turmeric 2½ tbsp/40 ml vegetable oil	See basic method opposite.
daffodil yellow	4 tsp/20 ml turmeric 2½ tbsp/40 ml vegetable oil	See basic method opposite. Yields a more intense yellow.
red (pink-mauve)	1 tsp/5 ml dried alkanet root 2–4 tbsp/30–60 ml vegetable oil	See basic method opposite.
pale pink	1 tsp/5 ml dried alkanet root 5 tbsp/75 ml vegetable oil	See basic method opposite. When starting with a white soap base, eliminate the tablespoon of glycerin required in those recipes to achieve this color.
cranberry red (purple)	2–4 tsp/10–20 ml dried alkanet root 4 tbsp/60 ml vegetable oil	Crush the alkanet root with a mortar and pestle to release the dye. Place in a heat-proof bowl with the oil over a pan of simmering water. Infuse for 30 to 45 minutes, or until the required depth of color is achieved. Strain through a coffee filter or tea strainer.
green	2 tsp/10 ml spirulina powder 4 tbsp/60 ml vegetable oil	See basic method opposite.
dark green	4 tbsp/60 ml yellow base color (see first yellow recipe above) blue/German chamomile essential oil	Add drops of essential oil to the base color until the desired intensity is reached.
blue	½ tsp/2.5 ml blue/German chamomile essential oil ½ tsp/2.5 ml blue cypress essential oil 4 tsp/20 ml vegetable oil	Measure the ingredients and mix together. Bottle and use when needed.

aroma profiles

Listed below is a brief description of the aroma and blending companions for all the essential oils and absolutes used in the recipes. Many, if not all, of these can be purchased at any good essential oil distributor (see pages 124–125 for list of suppliers). You can use this information to create your own personal blends. Some oils and absolutes are best avoided if you have highly sensitive skin, suffer from asthma or allergies, or are pregnant. Please check the ingredients lists of individual recipes against the bulleted cautions in these profiles before making any recipes for the first time. Also review the Safety and Hygiene box on page 21, and if you experience an adverse reaction and symptoms persist, seek medical advice and mention that aromatherapy products have been used.

AMBRETTE SEED
(*Abelmoschus moschatus*)
AROMA: floral, musky, rich, and sweet.
BLENDING COMPANIONS: patchouli, neroli, rose, clary sage, cypress.

ANGELICA SEED
(*Angelica archangelica L*)
AROMA: light, fresh strong peppery scent.
BLENDING COMPANIONS: vetiver, citruses, clary sage, oakmoss, sage, patchouli.
● Avoid during pregnancy.

ATLAS CEDARWOOD
(*Cedrus atlantica*)
AROMA: warm, sweet, woody, soft.
BLENDING COMPANIONS: mimosa, rose, frankincense, bergamot, clary sage, rosemary, ylang ylang, juniper berry, jasmine florals, resins.
● Avoid during pregnancy.

BASIL (*Ocimum basilicum*)
AROMA: fresh, light, sweet, spicy, with a balsamic undertone.
BLENDING COMPANIONS: oakmoss, lime, clary sage, geranium, bergamot, vetiver.
● Avoid during pregnancy.

BAY (*Pimenta racemosa*)
AROMA: fresh, spicy, sweet balsamic undertone.
BLENDING COMPANIONS: ylang ylang, rosemary, lavender, lavandin, citruses, spices, petitigrain.

BENZOIN (*Styrax benzoin*)
AROMA: sweet, balsamic, vanillalike.
BLENDING COMPANIONS: sandalwood, rose, jasmine, frankincense, myrrh, coriander, juniper, spices, lemon.

BERGAMOT (*Citrus bergamia*)
AROMA: fresh, sweet, fruity, lively, citrus with a hint of spice.
BLENDING COMPANIONS: jasmine, neroli, chamomile, coriander, geranium, florals.
● It is advisable to use FCF bergamot (furocoumarin-free).

BLACKCURRANT BUD (*Ribes nigrum*)
AROMA: spicy-woody, like the fruit.

BLENDING COMPANIONS: sandalwood, bergamot, citruses, galangal, vanilla.

BLACK PEPPER (*Piper nigrum*)
AROMA: warm, spicy, dry, woody, fresh.
BLENDING COMPANIONS: florals (in small amounts), rosemary, frankincense, lavender, spices, sandalwood.
● Avoid during pregnancy.

BLUE/GERMAN CHAMOMILE
(*Matricaria recutica*)
AROMA: intensely sweet, herbaceous, with fruity-fresh undertone.
BLENDING COMPANIONS: geranium, neroli, clary sage, rose, citruses, patchouli, lavender, ylang ylang, jasmine, bergamot, labdanum.
● Can cause skin irritation. Use low dilution of 0.5%.

CARDOMOM (*Elettaria cardamomum*)
AROMA: rich-aromatic, spicy, warm, floral undertones, sweet, hint of eucalyptus.
BLENDING COMPANIONS: geranium, cinnamon, ginger, ylang ylang, rose, jasmine, cedarwood, cloves, citruses, lavender, neroli, frankincense.

CARNATION (*Dianthus caryophyllus*)
AROMA: clovelike, honeylike, herbaceous, sweet, and heavy.
BLENDING COMPANIONS: clary sage, lavender, ylang ylang, frankincense, cedarwood, citruses, coriander, petitgrain.

CARROT SEED (*Daucus carota*)
AROMA: woody, earthy, warm, sweet, and fresh initial notes, fruity, sharp, spicy.
BLENDING COMPANIONS: citruses, frankincense, geranium, spices, cedarwood, mimosa.

CINNAMON LEAF
(*Cinnamomum zeylanicum*)
AROMA: hot and spicy, dry and tenacious.
BLENDING COMPANIONS: field mint, spices, ylang ylang, rose, citruses, cedarwood, sandalwood, benzoin.
● Can cause skin irritation. Use leaf, as bark is highly irritating.

CITRONELLA
(*Cymbopagon nardus L herbae*)
AROMA: woody-sweet, fresh, grassy. Java-type is sweeter in note. Ceylonese variety is cruder and often adulterated.
BLENDING COMPANIONS: pine, sweet orange, cedarwood, geranium, bergamot, lemon, palmarosa.
● Avoid during pregnancy.

CLARY SAGE (*Salvia sclarea*)
AROMA: sweet, haylike, spicy, nutty.
BLENDING COMPANIONS: juniper berry, sandalwood, cedarwood, lavender, coriander, frankincense, citruses, bergamot, cardomom, geranium.
● Avoid during pregnancy.

CLOVE BUD (*Eugenia aromatica*)
AROMA: sweet, spicy, strong fruity-fresh top note.
BLENDING COMPANIONS: ylang ylang, citruses, vanilla, rose, spices, geranium, bergamot, clary sage, bay, lavandin.

CORIANDER (*Coriandrum sativum*)
AROMA: sharp, woody-spicy top note, floral-balsamic undertone, light, sweet, slightly musky.
BLENDING COMPANIONS: juniper berry, frankincense, citruses, spices, jasmine, pine, petitgrain, sandalwood, clary sage, neroli, ginger, cinnamon, jasmin.

CYPRESS (*Cupressus sempervirens*)
AROMA: sweet, balsamic, smoky.
BLENDING COMPANIONS: citruses, lavender, cedarwood, labdanum, ambrette seed, sandalwood, pine, clary sage, juniper berry, benzoin, cardomom.

EUCALYPTUS (*Eucalyptus globulus*)
AROMA: camphorous, woody, strong with a woody-sweet undertone.
BLENDING COMPANIONS: lemon, rosemary, cedarwood, lavender, peppermint, clove, lemongrass, spike lavender.

FIELD MINT/CORNMINT
(*Mentha arvensis*)
AROMA: bitter-sweet, minty, fresh, strong, woody undertone.

BLENDING COMPANIONS: rosemary, eucalyptus, mints, benzoin, neroli, tuberose, vanilla, hyacinth, oakmoss, mandarin, myrtle, ylang ylang, rose, linden blossom, lavender.

FIR NEEDLE (Abies alba)
AROMA: sweet-balsamic, rich, fresh, soft, forestlike.
BLENDING COMPANIONS: oakmoss, juniper berry, patchouli, cedarwood, citruses, rosemary, frankincense, lavender, pine.

FRANKINCENSE (Boswellia carteri)
AROMA: warm, hint of lemon and camphor, balsamic, rich, deep, sweet, woody, with incenselike overtones.
BLENDING COMPANIONS: geranium, pepper, citruses, spices, lavender, fir, basil, cedarwood, rose, vetiver, cypress, ho leaf, sandalwood, juniper berry, neroli, mimosa.
• Avoid during pregnancy.

GALANGAL (Alpinia officinarum)
AROMA: spicy-woody, fresh-camphorous, warm undertone, rich and spicy body.
BLENDING COMPANIONS: cinnamon, sage, citruses, blackcurrant bud, pine, rosemary, myrtle, patchouli.

GERANIUM (Pelargonium graveolens)
Associated oils include geranium bourbon.
AROMA: rose, sweet, minty.
BLENDING COMPANIONS: black pepper, patchouli, petitgrain, vetiver, bergamot, coriander, clary sage, juniper berry, sandalwood, jasmine, lavender, sage, neroli, clove, citruses, rose.

GINGER (Zingiber officinale)
AROMA: woody, spicy, slightly green, fresh, warm, pungent, undertone is rich, tenacious, and sweet.
BLENDING COMPANIONS: coriander, citruses, cedarwood, ho leaf, neroli, orange, frankincense, cinnamon, petitgrain, vetiver, ylang ylang, rose, lime, sandalwood.
• Can cause skin irritation.

GRAPEFRUIT (Citrus × paradisi)
AROMA: sweet, fresh, citrus, bright, sharp.
BLENDING COMPANIONS: geranium, spices, cardomom, lemon, palmarosa, lavender, neroli, carrot seed, jasmine, coriander, petitgrain, pine, juniper berry, cypress.

HELICHRYSUM (Helichrysum angustifolium var. italicum)
AROMA: honeylike, rich, fruity, deep, tealike undertone.
BLENDING COMPANIONS: lavender, geranium, citruses, rose, clary sage, chamomile, mimosa, oakmoss.

HO LEAF (Cinnamomum camphora)
AROMA: floral, sweet, camphorous, soft.
BLENDING COMPANIONS: rosemary, neroli, florals, citruses. Blends with most oils.

HYACINTH (Hyacinthus orientalis)
AROMA: intensely sweet, green, floral.
BLENDING COMPANIONS: neroli, rose, jasmine, benzoin, vanilla, ylang ylang.

JASMINE (Jasminum officinale)
AROMA: rich, floral, powerful, warm, highly diffusive, tealike undertone.
BLENDING COMPANIONS: rose, citruses, clary sage, sandalwood, florals, oakmoss. Blends with most oils.

JUNIPER BERRY (Juniperus communis)
AROMA: woody, balsamic, sweet, fresh, peppery overtone.
BLENDING COMPANIONS: petitgrain, fir, geranium, neroli, bergamot, rosemary, cedarwood, sandalwood, frankincense, cypress, clary sage, pine, citruses, vetiver, oakmoss, lavandin.
• Avoid during pregnancy.

LAVENDER (Lavandula)
There are many different varieties of lavender and associated oils.
AROMA: 'Alpine'/fine – harsh-floral, very sweet; 'High altitude' – herbaceous, floral, wood-earthy notes; 'rare/fine' – sweetly balsamic, floral; 'Maillette' – woody-green-herbaceous, tough.
BLENDING COMPANIONS: oakmoss, citruses, patchouli, rosemary, clary sage, pine, bergamot, clove, coriander, frankincense, geranium, mimosa, neroli, petitgrain, rose, florals, cedarwood, vetiver.

LEMON (Citrus limon)
AROMA: sweet, fresh, sharp, clean, citrusy.
BLENDING COMPANIONS: lavender, citruses, oakmoss, Roman chamomile, eucalyptus, frankincense, juniper berry, myrrh, neroli, petitgrain, rose, benzoin, sandalwood, ylang ylang, basil, geranium.
• Can cause skin irritiation.

LEMONGRASS (Cymbopogon citratus and C. flexuosus)
AROMA: citratus – lemony, fresh, light, sweet; flexuosus – lemony, slightly bitter, earthy undertone. Both have a fresh grassy, lemon-herbal and tealike scent.
BLENDING COMPANIONS: geranium, lavender, jasmine, clary sage, bergamot, Roman chamomile, palmarosa, cardomom, rosemary, petitgrain, eucalyptus, patchouli, clove, carnation, narcissus, tuberose. rose.
• Can cause skin irritiation.

LIME, DISTILLED (Citrus aurantifolia)
AROMA: sharp, fresh, citrus, tart, sweet.
BLENDING COMPANIONS: clary sage, rosemary, lavender, neroli, citronella, citruses, ylang ylang, petitgrain.

LINDEN BLOSSOM (Tilia europa)
AROMA: dry, green, herbaceous, clean, cucumberlike.
BLENDING COMPANIONS: vanilla, tuberose, jasmine, narcissus, orange, mimosa, oakmoss, English rose phytol, myrtle, myrrh, mandarin, ylang ylang, hyacinth, neroli, benzoin.

MAGNOLIA (Magnolia grandiflora)
AROMA: delicate, sweet, reminiscent of rose, violet, and orangeflowers.
BLENDING COMPANIONS: rose, violet, neroli, vanilla.

MANDARIN (Citrus reticulata)
Associated oils include green, red, yellow.
AROMA: sweet, floral, citrus.
BLENDING COMPANIONS: neroli, cinnamon, clove, nutmeg, rosemary, geranium, coriander, petitgrain, rose, citruses.

MAY CHANG (Litsea cubeba)
AROMA: intense lemony, fresh, fruity, soft.
BLENDING COMPANIONS: citruses, rosemary, ho leaf, neroli, rosewood.

MIMOSA (Acacia dealbata)
AROMA: rich, floral, woody, sweet, spicy.
BLENDING COMPANIONS: jasmine, geranium, ylang ylang, citruses, Roman chamomile, clary sage, coriander, neroli, sandalwood, cedarwood, petitgrain, rose, lavender.

MYRRH (Commiphora myrrha)
AROMA: deep-spicy, very rich, warm, balsamic, aromatic.
BLENDING COMPANIONS: lemongrass, coriander, cypress, oakmoss, patchouli, cedarwood, frankincense, palmarosa, benzoin, mandarin, mints, florals, lavender, spices, sandalwood.
• Avoid during pregnancy.

MYRTLE (Myrtus communis)
AROMA: sweet, herbaceous, spicy, clear fresh body note.
BLENDING COMPANIONS: bay, ginger, lime, lavender, bergamot, clary sage, clove, rosemary.

NARCISSUS (Narcissus poeticus)
AROMA: green, sweet, herbaceous, faint floral undertone; 'des plaines' – floral-sweet, mild and rich; 'des montagnes' – powerful, sharp, green.
BLENDING COMPANIONS: jasmine, neroli, clove, sandalwood, mimosa, rose, spices, ambrette seed.

NEROLI BIGARADE
(*Citrus aurantium* var. *amara*)
AROMA: floral, delicate, rich, warm, sweet-bitter undertone.
BLENDING COMPANIONS: rose, clary sage, Roman chamomile, coriander, citruses, geranium, lavender, ylang ylang, jasmine. Blends well with most oils.

NUTMEG (*Myristica fragrans*)
AROMA: spicy, warm, sweet, musky.
BLENDING COMPANIONS: coriander, lavandin, mandarin, oakmoss, geranium, sweet orange, lime, petitgrain, spices, bay, clary sage, rosemary, florals, woods, citruses, neroli, ylang ylang.

OAKMOSS (*Evernia prunastri*)
AROMA: earthy, mossy, barklike.
BLENDING COMPANIONS: juniper berry, lavender, pine, vetiver, florals, cedarwood, clary sage, citruses, patchouli, pine, petitgrain, bergamot, coriander.

PALMAROSA
(*Cymbopogon martinii* var. *motia*)
AROMA: green, fresh, lemony, strong, sweet, floral, rosy undertones.
BLENDING COMPANIONS: sandalwood, lavender, citruses, cedarwood, coriander, Roman chamomile, ylang ylang, ho leaf, geranium, florals, woods.

PATCHOULI (*Pogostemon cablin*)
AROMA: earthy, rich, sweet, herbal.
BLENDING COMPANIONS: geranium, clove, sandalwood, cedarwood, rose, lavender, myrrh, neroli, clary sage, oakmoss, ambrette seed, vetiver.

PEPPERMINT (*Mentha piperita*)
AROMA: camphorous, grassy-minty.
BLENDING COMPANIONS: mints, eucalyptus, rosemary, benzoin, citruses, lavender.

PETITGRAIN BIGARADE (*Citrus aurantium* ssp. *amara*)
AROMA: fresh-floral, citrus.
BLENDING COMPANIONS: citruses, lavender, rosemary, bergamot, jasmine, benzoin, neroli, palmarosa, clove, pine.

PETITGRAIN MANDARIN
(*Citrus reticulata blanca*)
AROMA: intensely rich, sweet, and musty.
BLENDING COMPANIONS: citruses, neroli, florals, cedarwood, sandalwood, vanilla.

PINE NEEDLE (*Pinus sylvestris*)
AROMA: balsamic, dry, and strong with a camphorous undertone.
BLENDING COMPANIONS: lemon, juniper berry, cedarwood, rosemary, bergamot, tea tree, cypress, frankincense, eucalyptus, lavender.
● Can cause skin irritation.

ROMAN CHAMOMILE
(*Chamaemelum nobile*)
AROMA: applelike, dry, fresh, sweet-herbaceous, fruity, warm, tea-leaf like.
BLENDING COMPANIONS: jasmine, neroli, rose, lavender, geranium, oakmoss, patchouli, clary sage, ylang ylang.

ROSE (*Rosaceae*)
AROMA: *Rosa centifolia* (rose Maroc)–rich and sweet, rosy with a strong, honeylike scent. When diluted it is delicate, sweet, balsamic with a faint woody undertone; *Rosa damascena* (rose otto) – deep, sweet-floral, warm, slightly spicy, rich with spicy, honeylike notes; English rose phytol – intensely sweet, delicate, light, warm, dusky.
BLENDING COMPANIONS: All three types of rose blend well with most oils including frankincense, petitgrain, vanilla, florals, and citruses.

ROSEMARY (*Rosmarinus officinalis*)
AROMA: strong, minty, forestlike, woody, balsamic, dry, herbaceous, bittersweet.
BLENDING COMPANIONS: peppermint, lavender, cedarwood, cinnamon, frankincense, citronella, spices, pine.
● Avoid during pregnancy.

SANDALWOOD (*Santalum album*)
AROMA: sweet-woody, soft, deep, balsamic.
BLENDING COMPANIONS: rose, lavender, clove, tuberose, black pepper, bergamot, oakmoss, geranium, mimosa, myrrh, jasmine, vetiver, patchouli, benzoin, vetiver, cypress, frankincense, juniper berry, pine, ylang ylang.

SPIKE LAVENDER (*Lavandula latifolia*)
AROMA: fresh, herbaceous, camphorous.
BLENDING COMPANIONS: clover, petitgrain, pine, rosemary, juniper berry, eucalyptus, bergamot, patchouli, fir, lavender.

SPIKENARD (*Nardostachys jatamansi*)
AROMA: spicy, heavy, sweet, woody, earthy, strong, herbal.
BLENDING COMPANIONS: lavender, vetiver, spices, fir, citruses, cedarwood, oakmoss, patchouli, vetiver, ginger, cardamom, pine.

STAR ANISE (*Illicium verum*)
AROMA: intensely sweet, licoricelike, spicy, warm.
BLENDING COMPANIONS: sweet orange, mints, pine, rose, lavender.
● Avoid during pregnancy.

SWEET ORANGE (*Citrus sinensis*)
AROMA: refreshing, sweet, light, lively.
BLENDING COMPANIONS: lavender, myrrh, rosemary, clary sage, coriander, citruses, frankincense, patchouli, geranium, spices.

TAGETES/MEXICAN MARIGOLD
(*Tagetes patula* and *T. minuta*)
AROMA: fruity and powerful top note, herbaceous, and sharp.
BLENDING COMPANIONS: lavender, jasmine, bergamot, lemon, orange.
● Can cause skin irritation.

TANGERINE (*Citrus reticulata*)
AROMA: sweet, fresh, orangelike, sharp.
BLENDING COMPANIONS: cinnamon, neroli, nutmeg, clove, citruses, lemongrass, rose, coriander, petitgrain, geranium, blue/German chamomile, rosemary.

TEA TREE (*Melaleuca alternifolia*)
AROMA: warm-spicy, camphorous.
BLENDING COMPANIONS: geranium, lavender, rosemary, spices (especially clove and nutmeg), oakmoss, clary sage, pine, eucalyptus, lemon, lavandin.

TUBEROSE ABSOLUTE
(*Polianthes tuberosa*)
AROMA: heavy-floral, very sweet, spicy.
BLENDING COMPANIONS: vanilla, mint, frankincense, tangerine, coriander, cinnamon, cardamom, nutmeg, black pepper, ginger, orange, jasmine, mimosa, neroli, rose, linden blossom, narcissus.

VANILLA (*Vanilla planifolia*)
AROMA: rich, sweet, creamy, smooth, balsamic, vanilla.
BLENDING COMPANIONS: spices, sandalwood, vetiver, balsams, florals, woods, ylang ylang, frankincense, citruses, rose, jasmine, cedarwood.

VETIVER (*Vetiveria zizanioides*)
AROMA: earthy-woody, rich, smoky, sweet molasseslike undertones.
BLENDING COMPANIONS: mimosa, oakmoss, rose, jasmine, patchouli, petitgrain, ylang ylang, citruses, sandalwood, clary sage, lavender.

YLANG YLANG
(*Cananga odorata* var. *genuina*)
AROMA: cloying, very sweet, soft, heavy, slightly spicy, floral, balsamic, tropical.
BLENDING COMPANIONS: geranium, citruses, florals, vetiver, black pepper, ho leaf, mimosa, rose, jasmine, tuberose.

Safety and Hygiene

❖ Never take essential oils internally.

❖ Keep essential oils out of the reach of children and away from the eyes. Do not rub your eyes after handling essential oils or absolutes.

❖ Do not eat, drink, or smoke without washing your hands after working with essential oils.

❖ Citrus oils, especially bergamot, increase the skin's sensitivity to ultra-violet light. Do not use on the skin shortly before exposure to sunlight (or a tanning bed) as they may cause unsightly pigmentation and increase the risk of sunburn.

❖ Never use an essential oil or absolute about which you can find little or no information.

❖ Do not apply essential oils directly to the skin; always dilute them in a base oil, as undiluted oils can be extremely irritating to the skin. If you have sensitive skin, it is advisable to carry out a patch test before using an essential oil for the first time. Simply rub a little oil in the crook of your arm and leave for 24 hours. If no irritation occurs, the oil is safe to use.

❖ Avoid the following essential oils if you have sensitive skin: blue/German chamomile, cinnamon leaf, ginger, lemon, lemongrass, pine needle, tagetes.

❖ Skin applications of certain essential oils are best avoided during pregnancy. Refer to the cautions given in the aroma profiles (pages 18–20) or any good aromatherapy manuals.

❖ Don't store essential oils in plastic, as some oils dissolve plastic.

❖ Prepare your surfaces by cleaning with boiling water and disinfectant.

❖ Wear disposable gloves (available at chemists and drug stores) when making soap and handling essential oils.

❖ Sterilize all utensils and storage bottles or dispensers.

❖ Keep your soapmaking equipment separate from utensils used for preparing and cooking food, and do not reuse the equipment for cooking purposes.

❖ Store base products such as creams and lotions in a cool, dark cupboard or refrigerator (note that some preservatives crystallize at low temperatures).

❖ When using base products such as hydrolats or plant milks, replace the cap as soon as possible to prevent bacteria from contaminating the product.

whipped cream soaps

jemina

This recipe uses a base color with alkanet root, which contains a red pigment that gives this soap a beautiful hue, redolent of a **soft**, Swedish pink. The addition of **honey** creates a **delicate**, soft texture. The scent is pure rose.

yield: 4 soaps

ingredients

31 drops rose otto essential oil or rose absolute

1½ tbsp/22.5 ml red base color (see p.17)

1½ cups/110g soap flakes

10 tbsp/150 ml rosewater

½ tbsp/7.5 ml honey

dried pink rosebuds for decoration (one for each soap)

preparation

First, add the rose oil to the red base color and put aside. Measure out the other ingredients and set aside. Grease a rectangular mold. Following the instructions on page 14, place the soap flakes, rosewater, and honey in the top part of a double boiler over simmering water to melt. Stir occasionally with a chopstick or skewer until the mixture appears less fluid and more soaplike. Remove the boiler from the heat. Pour in the scented red base color and whisk vigorously by hand or with an electric beater until the mixture resembles whipped cream.

Spoon the pink-colored mixture quickly into the mold, and smooth the top with a spoon dipped in hot water. Leave in a warm place for an hour. Check for firmness and turn out of the mold on to waxed paper as soon as the soap is solid enough. Divide into four blocks (see page 15) or use a heart-shaped cookie cutter to cut out individual soaps.

finishing touches

For a pretty effect, while the soap is still sufficiently soft, place one rosebud in the middle of each soap. Leave overnight in a warm place, then in the morning transfer to a container lined with waxed paper. Check daily. The soap should be ready in two to three weeks.

white jungle

May chang, known for its fragrant flowers, imparts an intensely **lemony** aroma. Oriental ho leaf adds a touch of camphor, while the basil gives a spicy tang. The scent is **delicate** and yet refreshing, with a sweet, **floral**, and woody character.

yield: 4 soaps
ingredients
1½ cups/110 g soap flakes
10 tbsp/150 ml rosewater
1 tbsp/15 ml glycerin
1 tbsp/15 ml sunflower oil
15 drops lemon essential oil
6 drops ho leaf essential oil
6 drops may chang essential oil
4 drops basil essential oil

preparation

Following the instructions on page 14, place a double boiler on the stove and heat to a simmer. Grease a rectangular mold. Put the soap flakes, rosewater, and glycerin into the top part of the double boiler to melt. Add the essential oils drop by drop to the sunflower oil.

When the melting soap flakes resemble a lumpy paste, stir with a chopstick or metal skewer. Quickly take the double boiler off the heat. Whisk vigorously by hand or with an electric beater until the soap looks frothy. Pour the sunflower oil, scented with essential oils, into the soap mixture. The mixture will turn white.

As soon as the consistency feels smooth and there appear to be no more lumps, pour or spoon out the mixture into the waiting mold. Smooth the surface, cover, and leave in a warm place.

finishing touches

As soon as the soap has sufficiently hardened (between 30 minutes to an hour), turn it out of the mold and cut it into four (see page 15). Wrap in waxed paper and place in a cool, dark cupboard to set. The soap will be ready in 24 hours. However, this recipe does benefit from a longer setting time so, if possible, leave for one to three weeks.

sanskrit

The combination of frankincense, **heady** geranium, cedarwood, and rose creates a floral, **woody**, and resinous scent. The addition of paprika gives this soap a beautiful, **peachy** rose color.

yield: 6 soaps
ingredients
3 cups/225 g soap flakes
13 tbsp/195 ml rosewater
2 tbsp/30 ml glycerin
1 tsp/5 ml powdered paprika
1 tbsp/15 ml sunflower oil
25 drops geranium essential oil
25 drops atlas cedarwood essential oil
6 drops frankincense/ olibanum essential oil

preparation

Following the instructions on page 14, place a double boiler on the stove and heat to a simmer. Grease a rectangular mold. Add the soap flakes, rosewater, and glycerin to the top half of the boiler and melt. Add the paprika to the sunflower oil and mix well. Stir the melted soap with a chopstick or skewer. As the soap starts to congeal, keep stirring and, as soon as most of the rosewater and glycerin have been incorporated, remove from the stove. Add the sunflower oil mixed with the paprika, and the essential oils.

Whisk vigorously by hand or with an electric beater until the mixture looks smooth. Spoon into the mold and smooth the surface with the spoon dipped in hot water. Leave in a warm place. After about 45 minutes to an hour, test for firmness. If the mixture looks and feels firm to the touch, turn out the soaps and divide into six blocks (see page 15).

finishing touches

Press a pattern on to the top of the soaps with a wood stamp or petit-four cutter. Press gently but firmly in the middle of each soap. Let harden in a cool, dark place for about two to three weeks before use.

citrus smoothy

A mixture of natural paprika and turmeric in the base color creates a lovely, frothy, **orange** juice shade. The soap has a light, airy texture and the combination of invigorating citrus oils creates a lively, bright, sweet, **fresh**, and **sharp** scent.

yield: 4 soaps

ingredients

1½ cups/110 g soap flakes
¼ cup/25 g white beeswax pellets
1 tbsp/15 ml glycerin
1 tbsp/15 ml orange base color (see p.17)
10 tbsp/150 ml bottled water
15 drops sweet orange essential oil
15 drops grapefruit essential oil
15 drops lemon essential oil
15 drops distilled lime essential oil

preparation

Following the instructions on page 14, place a double boiler on the stove and heat to a simmer. Grease a rectangular mold. Put the soap flakes, beeswax pellets, glycerin, orange base color, and water in the top half of the double boiler over the heat. Stir with a skewer or chopstick as the mixture starts to melt.

Check the soap and give it a brisk stir. When it looks well blended, remove from the heat. Add the essential oils and whisk vigorously by hand or with an electric beater.

When the soap looks creamy and frothy, quickly spoon into the waiting mold and smooth the surface with the back of the spoon. Leave in a warm, dry place for one to one-and-a-half hours. Turn out of the mold and cut into four blocks (see page 15). Place on waxed paper and return to a warm area overnight.

finishing touches

To add a decorative detail, press a petit-four cutter gently but firmly in the middle of the soap to make a sharp indentation. With the end of a paintbrush make an outline inside the cutter shape so that an imprint is made. Return to a dry spot again for two to three days, then let harden in a cool, dark area for one to three weeks.

chinese tea garden

The **darjeeling** tea gives this soap a gentle peach tone.
The exotic scents of **ylang ylang** and monoi de Tahiti are
softened by the addition of **rose**. The soap itself is a little
harder than the other whipped cream soaps.

yield: 4 soaps
ingredients
1½ cups/110 g soap flakes
6 tbsp/90 ml monoi de Tahiti
4 tbsp/60 ml bottled water
1 tbsp/15 ml glycerin
1 tbsp/15 ml sweet almond oil
3 tbsp/45 ml darjeeling tea infusion
15 drops rose essential oil
10 drops ylang ylang essential oil
6 drops benzoin liquid resin

preparation

darjeeling tea infusion

2 darjeeling tea bags or 2 tsp/10ml loose darjeeling tea,
5 tbsp/75 ml bottled water

Place the tea bags or loose tea in the water. Heat in a
microwave for one minute on high. Alternatively, pour
5 tbsp/75 ml of boiling water on to the tea and let steep for
five minutes. Squeeze the tea bags well or strain the loose
tea to yield 3 tbsp/45 ml of liquid.

Place the soap flakes in the top part of a double boiler with
the monoi de Tahiti, over a simmering heat. Add the water,
glycerin, and sweet almond oil, followed by the tea infusion.
Grease a rectangular mold. With a chopstick or skewer, stir
the soap quickly in the pan. Remove from the heat once all
the ingredients have started to blend. Add the essential oils
and benzoin liquid resin and stir. With an electric beater or
hand whisk, beat until everything is well incorporated (see
page 14). Spoon into the mold and smooth the surface.
Cover and place in a warm spot. Leave for one-and-a-half
hours, then cut into four pieces (see page 15).

finishing touches

Place the soap on waxed paper and return to a warm area.
Leave overnight until firm. Harden for one to three weeks.

blossom trail

The combination of citrus and **lime** oils conjures up hot, **summer** days, homemade lemonade, and a gentle breeze. Images of lime trees laden with blossoms are evoked by its intense, refreshing, herbaceous, **sweet**, and **cool** aroma.

yield: 4 soaps

ingredients

1½ cups/110 g soap flakes

1 tbsp/15 ml lime blossom essential oil

1 tbsp/15 ml glycerin

10 tbsp/150 ml bottled water

10 drops lemon essential oil

10 drops distilled lime essential oil (or substitute lemon oil)

5 drops basil essential oil

4 drops linden blossom absolute

1 tsp/5 ml yellow base color (see p.17)

preparation

Following the instructions on page 14, heat a double boiler to a simmer. Measure out the ingredients and place the bottles of essential oils in sequence. Put the soap flakes in the top part of the double boiler with the lime blossom oil, glycerin, and water. While this is beginning to melt, grease a rectangular mold.

With a chopstick or skewer, stir the soap quickly in the pan. Once all the ingredients have started to blend, remove from the heat. Add the essential oils and absolute and stir. Make sure that all the ingredients are well incorporated. With a hand whisk or electric beater, whisk the soap, adding drops of the yellow base color as you go, to achieve a light, peachy tone. Alternatively, leave out the yellow base color for a pure white, creamy soap.

Once all the ingredients are whipped together, pour or spoon the soap into the prepared mold. Cover and let set in a warm place. Leave for one-and-a-half hours until set. Turn out of the mold and divide into four (see page 15).

finishing touches

Place on waxed paper and return to a warm area. Let harden for a couple of days. Then put in a dark, cool spot for a couple of weeks, and use as needed.

mint & lavender slice

This soap has a **creamy** middle sandwiched between two lavender-colored layers. The moisturizing **lather** feels really soft on the skin. The scent is **herbal**, floral, **balsamic**, sweet, and cool.

yield: 6 soaps

ingredients

first and third layer
follow basic whipped cream soap recipe (see p.14) for each layer

2 tbsp/30 ml rosehip essential oil

1 tsp/5 ml red base color (see p.17)

31 drops lavender essential oil

second layer
ingredients for basic whipped cream soap recipe (see p.14)

31 drops field mint/ cornmint essential oil

preparation

first layer

Following the instructions on page 14, place the soap flakes, water, glycerin, rosehip oil, and red base color in the top part of a double boiler over a simmering heat. Grease a rectangular mold. With a skewer or chopstick, stir briskly to incorporate the ingredients. When they have begun to melt, stir again. The mixture will take on a lumpy appearance. Take the pan off the heat, add the lavender essential oil, and begin whisking. The soap will fluff up quickly, making it quite light. As soon as everything looks smooth, quickly spoon into the mold. Smooth the surface and leave in a warm place for about an hour. Once the soap appears firm, you can add the second layer.

second layer

Repeat the process, adding the field mint/cornmint oil before whisking. After whipping up the soap, quickly spoon the second layer on top of the first. Smooth the surface and let solidify for about an hour in a warm place.

third layer

Repeat stage one. Place this third layer on top of the second layer. Leave in a warm area for one to two hours. Turn out on to waxed paper and slice into six blocks. Leave in a warm spot for three to four days. When firm, transfer to a cool, dark place for two to three weeks.

indonesian delight

Fragrant **lemongrass**, ginger, and **coriander**, classic ingredients of Indonesian cooking, are combined together with **kukui** nut oil and creamy scented vanilla. This exotic mix has a light citrus, warm, **spicy**, and refreshing scent.

yield: 4 soaps
ingredients
10 tbsp/150 ml bottled water
1½ cups/110 g soap flakes
2 tbsp/30 ml kukui nut oil
1 tbsp/15 ml cocoa butter
2 drops vanilla absolute
15 drops lemongrass essential oil
8 drops coriander essential oil
6 drops ginger essential oil

preparation

Following the instructions on page 14, place the water, soap flakes, and kukui nut oil in the top of a double boiler over simmering water. Put the cocoa butter in a microwavable bowl and place in a microwave for 30 seconds on a high heat, or in a small saucepan on top of the stove, to melt. Pour the melted cocoa butter into the soap mixture and stir. Grease a rectangular mold.

Once the soap mixture is blended and looking lumpy, remove from the heat. Add the absolute and essential oils, and beat vigorously by hand or with an electric beater. The soap will quickly start to thicken and look like whipped cream.

Quickly spoon the soap into the waiting mold. Smooth over the surface with a spoon, and place in a warm spot for about one to one-and-a-half hours. Turn the soap out of the mold and divide into four blocks (see page 15).

finishing touches

Place the freshly cut soaps on to waxed paper in a warm area overnight. Check and leave for a few days to harden. Then transfer to a cool, dark spot for a week to two weeks. The soaps should then be ready to use.

melting pot mosaic

When you have been making regular batches of soap, you will have some leftovers. Put aside small **soap slivers** to use in this recipe. There is no need to add scent as the soaps already have **aroma**.

yield: 6 soaps
ingredients
4½ cups/275 g leftover whipped cream soap slices
½ cup/125 ml bottled water
1¾ cups/225 g leftover colored glycerin slices cut into cubes

preparation

Place a double boiler on top of the stove to heat to a simmer. Place the leftover whipped cream soap slices and the water in the top half of the double boiler over the simmering water. Grease a rectangular mold. Place the glycerin soap cubes in the bottom of your mold so that they are evenly distributed. Stir the melting soap with a chopstick or skewer.

As soon as the soap has melted down (this can take a couple of hours) and is uniform in consistency, pour into the mold. You may have to stir quite vigorously toward the end until the last few lumps have melted.

Smooth over the top with a spoon dipped in hot water. Let set in a warm place for one-and-a-half hours. Turn out of the mold, and cut into six blocks (see page 15).

finishing touches

Place on waxed paper and put back in a warm spot for three to five days. When the soaps appear hard enough, transfer them, including the waxed paper, to a cool, dark place until set. Use as needed.

winter forest

The combination of **frankincense** and myrrh makes this a perfect Christmas soap, evoking winter evenings in front of a roaring **log** fire. The scent is green, **woody**, earthy, resinous, warm, **spicy**, and balsamic.

yield: 4 soaps
ingredients
1½ cups/110 g soap flakes
10 tbsp/150 ml bottled water
2 tbsp/30 ml sunflower oil
6 drops juniper berry essential oil
7 drops atlas cedarwood essential oil
5 drops spikenard essential oil
7 drops frankincense/ olibanum essential oil
6 drops myrrh essential oil
2 tsp/10 ml red base color (see p.17)

preparation

Following the instructions on page 14, place a double boiler half-full of water on top of the stove and heat to a simmer. Grease a rectangular mold. Add the soap flakes, water, and sunflower oil to the pan. Stir well with a spoon to incorporate all the ingredients. As the ingredients start to melt, stir briskly and, when the mixture resembles a lumpy paste, take the whole pan off the stove and add the essential oils. Whisk vigorously by hand or with an electric beater. The soap will start to resemble whipped cream.

Quickly spoon the mixture into the waiting mold. Pour the red base color over the soap and with a skewer trace lines in the soap and create swirly patterns, making sure that the oil is not sinking to the bottom of the mold. Smooth the surface and put in a warm place for about one to one-and-a-half hours to set.

finishing touches

Turn out of the mold, divide into four blocks (see page 15), and place on a sheet of waxed paper. Leave in a warm area overnight. Check and then leave in a warm place again for a couple of days to harden. Place in a dark, cool spot for a week to two weeks to settle, until ready for use.

sweet bees & coconut

Adding a few drops of **yellow** base color to this soap gives it a gentle, **moonlight** hue. It has a **sweet**, floral, **warm**, and **spicy** aroma. Its texture is slightly harder than that of the other whipped cream soaps.

yield: 4 soaps

ingredients

1½ cups/110 g soap flakes

2 tbsp/30 ml coconut oil

¼ cup/25 g white beeswax pellets

10 tbsp/150 ml bottled water

5 drops yellow base color (see p.17)

35 drops ylang ylang essential oil

4 drops coriander essential oil

preparation

Following the instructions on page 14, fill the bottom half of a double boiler half-full of water and heat to a simmer. Grease a rectangular mold. Put the soap flakes in the top part of the double boiler. Put the coconut oil and beeswax pellets in a microwavable bowl and melt in a microwave on high for 30 seconds. Keep checking and adding extra seconds until the oil and pellets have melted together. Alternatively, melt in a saucepan on the stove. Add the melted concoction to the soap flakes, followed by the water and the drops of yellow base color. With a chopstick or skewer, stir briskly to mix together. As soon as the mixture has melted and looks lumpy, remove from the heat and add the essential oils. With an electric beater or hand whisk, whip the soap until it looks frothy and creamy.

Spoon into the mold and smooth the surface with a spoon dipped in hot water. Place in a warm spot for about an hour. Turn out of the mold and divide into four blocks (see page 15).

finishing touches

Place on waxed paper and return to a warm area for a few days to harden. When sufficiently dry, move to a cool, dark spot for two weeks. The soaps will then be ready to use.

butterfly on a bush

A simple bar of soap is transformed into something delicate, beautiful, and fragrant with the addition of pale **pink**, soap butterflies, made with a shaped cookie cutter. A hint of mimosa and **hyacinth** gives this soap a **floral-woody**, sweet, bright, **balsamic** scent.

yield: 4 soaps

ingredients

soap base
1½ cups/110 g soap flakes

2 tbsp/30 ml passion flower oil

10 tbsp/150 ml bottled water

8 drops ylang ylang essential oil

5 drops benzoin liquid resin

5 drops mimosa absolute

5 drops hyacinth absolute

preparation
soap base

Following the instructions on page 14, place the soap flakes, passion flower oil, and water in the top part of a double boiler over simmering water. Stir well with a skewer or chopstick to make sure that all has been mixed well. Grease a rectangular mold. Stir the melting soap mixture briskly. When the mixture is lumpy, take the pan off the stove, and add the remaining essential oils and absolutes. Beat vigorously with a hand whisk or electric beater.

When the mixture resembles whipped cream, spoon into the waiting mold. Smooth the surface. Place in a warm area to set. After one to one-and-a-half hours, check for firmness and, if ready, turn out of the mold. Measure and divide into four blocks (see page 15). Place the soaps on waxed paper and return to a warm place to set.

ingredients

butterflies

¼ cup/50 g soap flakes

1 tbsp/15 ml rosehip essential oil

5 tbsp/75 ml bottled water

10 drops red base color (see p.17)

16 drops ylang ylang essential oil

butterflies

Place the soap flakes, rosehip oil, and water in the top part of a double boiler over simmering water. Stir to mix thoroughly and add the red base color to the mixture while on the stove. Whisk as before and add the ylang ylang oil. Spoon into a greased rectangular mold. After about half an hour, turn out on to waxed paper. Press out four butterflies with a butterfly-shaped cookie cutter.

finishing touches

With a paintbrush, brush the base of each butterfly with very hot water and press carefully on to the drying soaps made earlier. Let dry for a couple of days and then leave in a cool, dark place to harden. The soaps should be ready in two to three weeks.

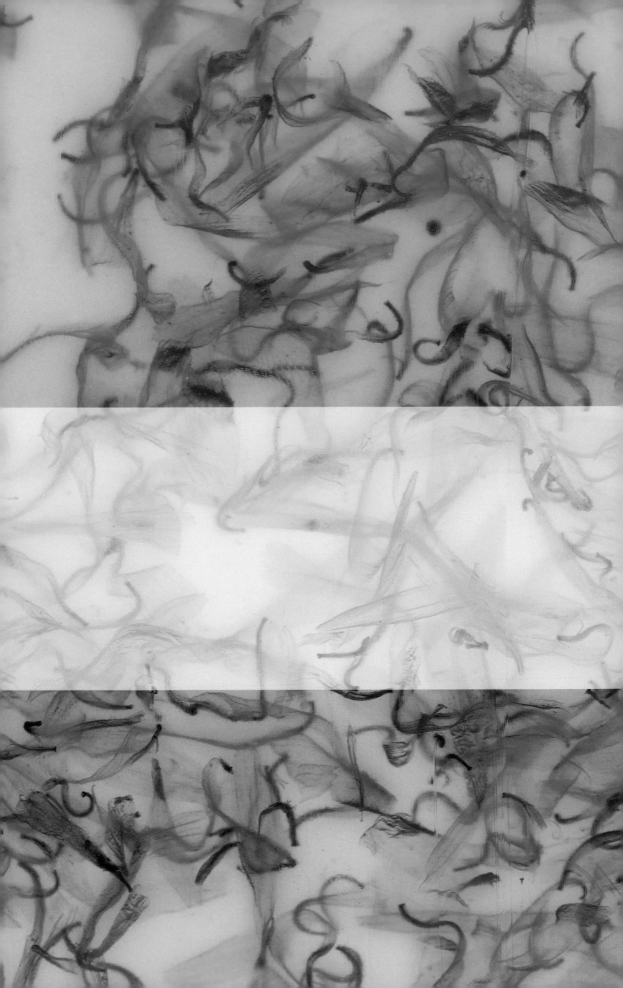

glycerin
soaps

herb garden

This soap is made from **rosemary**, lavender, Mexican **marigold**, and **basil**, a colorful quartet of herbs loved and grown in domestic gardens. It has a herbal, citrus, herbaceous, and **sweet-spicy** aromatic scent.

yield: 4 soaps
ingredients
2¼ cups/350 g grated block glycerin or glycerin soap pellets
7 drops basil essential oil
20 drops lavender true essential oil
20 drops lemon essential oil
10 drops tagetes essential oil
small pinch each of dried marigold flowers, lavender leaves, rosemary leaves
peel of half a dried lemon, cut into fine slivers

preparation

Following the instructions on page 14, fill the bottom half of a double boiler half-full of water and heat to a simmer. Place the grated glycerin or glycerin pellets in the top part of the double boiler. Leave the mixture to melt. Grease four shaped molds, or a retangular mold to make four soap blocks.

When all the glycerin has melted, remove from the heat, add the essential oils and stir. Pour the mixture into the molds.

finishing touches

Add the dried herbs and slices of dried lemon peel and stir gently but quickly with a chopstick or skewer, adjusting their position in the glycerin. Let cool for about one-and-a-half to two hours. Turn out of the molds. Measure and divide the soap into four, if not using shaped molds (see page 15). Place the soap blocks on waxed paper and let settle in a warm area. They are ready to use immediately.

chrysanthemum

The use of a **flower** mold and the yellow base color gives a **rich** dimension that contrasts with the transparency of the glycerin. The scent has a **floral** and lemony note, with warm-woody and **tealike** undertones.

yield: 4 soaps
ingredients
¾ cup/110 g grated block glycerin or glycerin soap pellets
10 drops yellow base color (see p.17)
6 drops may chang essential oil
5 drops citronella essential oil
10 drops palmarosa essential oil
10 drops Roman chamomile essential oil

preparation

Following the instructions on page 14, fill the bottom part of a double boiler half-full of water and heat to a simmer. Place the grated glycerin or glycerin pellets in the top part of the double boiler. Grease four flower-shaped flexible plastic molds, approximately 5 in (13 cm) in diameter.

Stir the melting glycerin with a skewer or chopstick, and add the yellow base color. Stir again, making sure that the color is distributed evenly throughout the melting glycerin. Once melted, remove from the heat and add the essential oils. Stir again to distribute the scent evenly and pour into the waiting molds. Leave for about one hour in a warm place to set. Turn out of the molds. Return to a warm place for a further 24 hours until ready for use.

a rose by any other name

The rose has traditionally been called the "queen of flowers" and rose oil is often thought of as the **queen** of essential oils. The red base color gives this soap a delicate **pink** tone. It has a deep, sweet, **rich**, tenacious floral rose scent.

yield: 6 soaps
ingredients
¾ cup/110 g grated block glycerin or glycerin soap pellets
20 drops red base color (see p.17)
24 drops rose Maroc essential oil or other rose essential oil

preparation

Following the instructions on page 14, fill the bottom half of a double boiler half-full of water and heat to a simmer. Place the grated glycerin or glycerin pellets in the top half of the double boiler to melt. Grease six rose-shaped flexible plastic molds, approximately 3 in (7.5 cm) in diameter, or a rectangular mold.

Stir the melting glycerin with a skewer or chopstick. Add the red base color and stir again, making sure that all the color has been evenly distributed. As soon as the ingredients have melted, remove from the heat and add the rose absolute. Stir well and pour evenly into the molds.

finishing touches

Let set for about one to one-and-a-half hours in a warm spot. Turn out of the molds. If you have used a rectangular mold, divide the block into six soaps (see page 15). Return to a warm place overnight until ready for use.

lavender & chamomile

Part of every **herb** garden, these plants are very gentle in their action and suitable for the most **sensitive** of skins. The addition of **oat** flakes and lavender flowers creates an unusual texture. This scent is **sweet**, floral, and herbaceous.

yield: 4 soaps
ingredients
2¾ cups/400 g grated block glycerin or glycerin soap pellets
½ tsp/2.5ml lavender essential oil
18 drops blue/German chamomile essential oil
35 drops lemon essential oil
good pinch of oat flakes
good pinch of lavender flowers

preparation

Following the instructions on page 14, fill the bottom half of a double boiler half-full of water and heat to a simmer. Place the grated glycerin or soap pellets in the top half of the double boiler to melt. Grease a rectangular mold.

When the glycerin has melted, stir well with a skewer or chopstick. Remove from the heat and add the essential oils. Pour into the waiting mold and add the oat flakes and lavender flowers. Stir gently.

finishing touches

Let set in a warm place for about one-and-a-half hours and then turn out of the mold. Measure and divide into four blocks (see page 15). Use immediately or store in a cool, dark place until required.

spice & mandarin grove

The fresh sweetness of mandarin contrasts well with the spiciness of **cinnamon** and soft woodiness of cedarwood. The color is **earthy-brown** and rich. The scent is spicy, soft, **woody**, fresh, sweet, and mobile.

yield: 4 soaps
ingredients
2¼ cups/350 g grated block glycerin or glycerin soap pellets
1 tsp/5 ml powdered cinnamon
1 tsp/5 ml mandarin essential oil
1 tsp/5 ml atlas cedarwood essential oil

preparation

Following the instructions on page 14, fill the double boiler half-full with water and place on top of the stove to heat to a simmer. Place the grated glycerin or glycerin pellets in the top half of the boiler over the heat. Grease a rectangular mold.

When the glycerin has melted, add the teaspoon of cinnamon and stir. The mixture will turn a wonderful, deep, earthy-brown. Take the whole pan off the heat and add the essential oils. Stir well with the skewer and then pour the mixture into the mold.

finishing touches

Leave in a warm place for about one to one-and-a-half hours to set. Turn out of the mold and divide into four blocks (see page 15). Use immediately or store in a cool, dark place until required.

marmalade

The vibrant mix of marigold flowers, orange base color, and **sweet** orange oil creates a **warm** tone with a speckled texture that resembles marmalade. This soap has a sweet, **bright** scent that uplifts the spirits.

yield: 4 soaps

ingredients

2¾ cups/400 g grated block glycerin or glycerin soap pellets
15 drops red base color (see p.17)
36 drops orange base color (see p.17)
1 tsp/5 ml sweet orange essential oil
good pinch dried of marigold flowers or dried zest of 1 orange

preparation

Following the instructions on page 14, fill the bottom part of a double boiler half-full of water and heat to a simmer. Place the grated glycerin or soap pellets in the top half of the double boiler to melt. Grease a rectangular mold.

When the glycerin has melted a little and is becoming liquid, add the base colors and stir with a skewer or chopstick, making sure that all the color is well incorporated. As soon as all the glycerin has melted, remove from the heat and add the essential oil. Pour into the waiting mold. Add the dried marigold flowers or orange zest to the liquid soap and stir to distribute evenly.

finishing touches

Leave for one-and-a-half hours in a warm place to set. Turn out of the mold and cut into four blocks (see page 15). The soap is ready for use.

cassis

This soap, with its wonderful **earthy** scent, will appeal to men and women alike. The fragrance of the **blackcurrant** buds cuts right through the scent. The use of **citrus** and **spicy** oils adds a fresh and **zingy** touch.

yield: 1 medium round-shaped soap

ingredients

1½ cups/225 g grated block glycerin or glycerin soap pellets

6 drops blackcurrant bud essential oil

6 drops FCF bergamot essential oil

18 drops galangal essential oil

18 drops sandalwood essential oil

6 drops oakmoss resin

1 sprig of rosemary

preparation

Following the instructions on page 14, fill the bottom half of a double boiler half-full with water and heat to a simmer. Place the grated glycerin or glycerin pellets in the top part of the double boiler and turn the heat down to low, so that the soap can melt gently. While the soap is melting, grease a round, flexible plastic mold. Check the soap and stir with a skewer or chopstick. When all the glycerin has melted and the mixture has a syrupy consistency, remove from the heat. Add the essential oils, stir and pour the soap into the mold.

Cover and place in a warm area. After one to one-and-a-half hours, the soap will have hardened sufficiently to turn it out of the mold.

finishing touches

At this stage, the soap is sufficiently hard, but still soft enough to make an impression on top. Press a wax seal into the middle of the soap to make an indentation, then add a sprig of rosemary, pressing firmly to fix it in place. You can use the soap immediately, or store in a cool, dark place.

If you use glycerin blocks, the color will be opaque. If you use soap pellets, the color will be clear with a green tint.

nanny's lemon soap

This soap embodies the spirit of my grandmother, a great lover of **flowers**. She always used lemon-shaped and scented soaps. It has a **delicate yellow** shade and a sweet, tangy, and **refreshing** scent.

yield: 4 soaps
ingredients
dried zest of half a lemon
2¾ cups/400 g grated block glycerin or glycerin soap pellets
5 drops yellow base color (see p.17)
2 tsp/10 ml lemon essential oil

preparation

First, peel the lemon very thinly with a zest peeler or a small, sharp knife. Then slice the peel carefully into slivers. Plunge them briefly into boiling water, then place in a warm oven to dry, until they are hard, but not brittle. This should take about five to ten minutes. Keep an eye on them after the first five minutes and more frequently after that.

Following the instructions on page 14, fill the bottom half of a double boiler half-full with water and heat to a simmer. Place the grated block glycerin or glycerin pellets in the top part of the double boiler to melt. Grease a rectangular mold. Add the drops of yellow base color and stir well with a skewer or chopstick. When all is incorporated and liquefied, remove from the heat and add the lemon oil. Stir well and pour into the mold.

finishing touches

Quickly add the dried lemon zest to the melted mixture. Stir with a skewer or chopstick so that a uniform amount of zest is distributed evenly throughout the soap. Leave in a warm place to set for about one to two hours. Turn out of the mold. Measure and cut into four blocks (see page 15). The soaps are ready to use immediately.

moroccan spice

This soap has a rich aroma and a warm, reddish-brown shade. The green **mandarin** and fir needles lend a clean, fresh **sharpness** that is balanced by the sweetness of ylang ylang and the warm and spicy tones of **anise**, bay, and clove.

yield: 4 soaps
ingredients
2¾ cups/400 g grated block glycerin or glycerin soap pellets
1 tsp/5ml red base color (see p.17)
30 drops frankincense/ olibanum essential oil
10 drops fir needle essential oil
7 drops bay essential oil
10 drops ylang ylang essential oil
20 drops green mandarin essential oil
3 drops clove bud essential oil
7 drops star anise essential oil
2 pinches powdered cinnamon

preparation

Following the instructions on page 14, fill the bottom half of a double boiler half-full with water and heat to a simmer. Place the grated glycerin or glycerin pellets into the top half of the double boiler to melt, adding the red base color. Line up the essential oils in sequence, and grease a rectangular mold. Stir the glycerin and as soon as it has melted, remove from the heat and add the essential oils, then the cinnamon. Stir. The mixture will turn a deep brick-brown color. Pour into the mold.

finishing touches

Leave for about one-and-a-half hours in a warm place and then turn out of the mold. Measure and cut into four blocks (see page 15). The soaps are ready for use.

so gentle

This soap is intended for those with **sensitive** skin. Macerated calendula oil and oat flakes combine to create a **soothing** blend. The color is **opaque** with a layered texture on the base. It has no scent.

yield: 4 soaps
ingredients
1½ cups/225 g grated block glycerin or glycerin soap pellets
1 tbsp/15 ml macerated calendula oil
⅓ cup/25 g small oat flakes

preparation

Following the instructions on page 14, fill the bottom half of a double boiler half-full with water and heat to a simmer. Place the grated glycerin or glycerin pellets in the top part of the boiler to melt. Grease a rectangular mold.

Stir the glycerin and, when it has melted, remove from the heat. Add the calendula oil and pour into the waiting mold. Add the oat flakes and stir. Leave for one-and-a-half hours in a warm place until firm and then turn out of the mold.

finishing touches

You will find that the oat flakes have sunk to the bottom, producing a graduated effect. Measure and cut the block of soap into four pieces (see page 15). The soaps are ready to use. Store in a dark, cool place if not using immediately.

red sky crescent moon

The **subtle** red of the background contrasts with the **translucent** yellow **glow** of the crescent moons. The scent is **sweet**, honeylike, **warm**, and floral.

yield: 4 soaps

ingredients

red sky
2¾ cups/400 g grated block glycerin or glycerin soap pellets

1 tsp/5 ml red base color (see p.17)

10 drops carnation absolute

crescent moon
1¼ cups/175 g grated block glycerin or glycerin soap pellets

18 drops benzoin liquid resin

17 drops ylang ylang extra essential oil

preparation
red sky

Following the instructions on page 14, fill the bottom half of a double boiler half-full with water and heat to a simmer. Place the grated glycerin or glycerin pellets in the pan to melt. Grease a rectangular mold. When the soap pellets have melted, remove from the heat. Stir in the red base color and mix thoroughly. Add the carnation absolute and stir well again. Pour carefully into the mold.

Put in a warm place for one to one-and-a-half hours until the soap has set. Turn out of the mold and divide into four blocks (see page 15). Place a crescent moon cutter in the middle of each soap and press down firmly. You will now have four crescents and four frames. (The leftover crescent soaps can be reused in the recipe on page 62.) Place the four frames back in the rectangular mold.

crescent moon

Melt the glycerin on the stove as above. When the soap has melted, add the benzoin and ylang ylang and stir. Pour into the empty crescent shapes in the soap frames that are in the rectangular mold. Let cool. From time to time press down gently on the crescent shapes to make sure that they are as level as possible with the frames. Let set again and turn out of the mold. Remove any foam around the crescent with a knife. The soaps are ready for use, or may be stored in a cool, dark place until required.

silent snow

This soap is a subtle, **opaque** color with just a **hint** of the palest **yellow**, evoking the cool, calm silence of a snow-covered landscape. The scent is rich, **sweet**, and intensely **floral**.

yield: 4 soaps
ingredients
1¼ cups/175 g grated block glycerin or glycerin soap pellets
6 drops linden blossom absolute
2 drops jasmine absolute
2 drops tuberose absolute
2 drops benzoin liquid resin

preparation

Following the instructions on page 14, fill the bottom half of a double boiler half-full with water and heat to a simmer. Place the grated glycerin or glycerin pellets in the top half of the pan to melt. Grease a rectangular mold.

Place the absolutes and liquid resin in sequence, ready for use. When the pellets have melted, remove from the heat, and add the absolutes and liquid resin. Stir well to incorporate the scents evenly. Pour into the waiting mold.

finishing touches

Leave for about one to one-and-a-half hours in a warm place and then turn out of the mold. Measure and cut into four blocks (see page 15). The soap is now ready for use. If you don't intend to use the soap immediately, store in a cool, dark place until needed.

hyacinth bowl

The scent of a bowl of hyacinths in **bloom** is intoxicating. This is a **luxurious** soap as hyacinth absolute is one of the more costly absolutes to purchase, but the richness of the sweet, **green-floral** scent is worth the indulgence.

yield: 4 soaps
ingredients
3 cups/450 g grated block glycerin or glycerin soap pellets
8 drops hyacinth absolute

preparation

Following the instructions on page 14, fill the bottom half of a double boiler half-full with water and heat to a simmer. Place the grated glycrin or glycerin pellets in the top half of the pan to melt. Stir the melting soap with a skewer or chopstick. Grease a rectangular mold.

When the mixture has melted, take the double boiler off the stove and add the absolute. Mix in thoroughly. Pour into the mold, and let set in a warm, dry place for about one to one-and-a-half hours.

finishing touches

Turn out the block from the mold and cut into four pieces (see page 15). If froth has formed on the soap, carefully slice it off as you square up the edges with a sharp knife. The soaps are ready to use.

wanderlust

Both the **cypress** and chamomile oils contain **blue** tones that turn this soap a soft **aquamarine**. The lavender imparts a **cool**, clear scent while the **pine** and cypress suggest a forest that is refreshing, woody, and herbaceous.

yield: 4 soaps
ingredients
2¾ cups/400 g grated glycerin block or glycerin soap pellets
30 drops spike lavender essential oil
10 drops Australian blue cypress essential oil
10 drops blue/German chamomile essential oil
20 drops red mandarin essential oil
21 drops lavender essential oil
2 drops oakmoss resin
20 drops pine needle essential oil

preparation

Following the instructions on page 14, fill the bottom half of a double boiler half-full with water and heat to a simmer. Place the grated glycerin or glycerin pellets in the top half of the double boiler to melt. Grease a rectangular mold.

Line up the essential oils in sequence, and give the melting glycerin a stir with a skewer or chopstick. Once all the glycerin has melted, remove from the heat and add the essential oils. Stir well and pour into the waiting mold.

finishing touches

Let set in a warm place for about one to one-and-a-half hours and then turn out of the mold. Measure and cut into four blocks (see page 15). Store in a cool, dark place until ready for use.

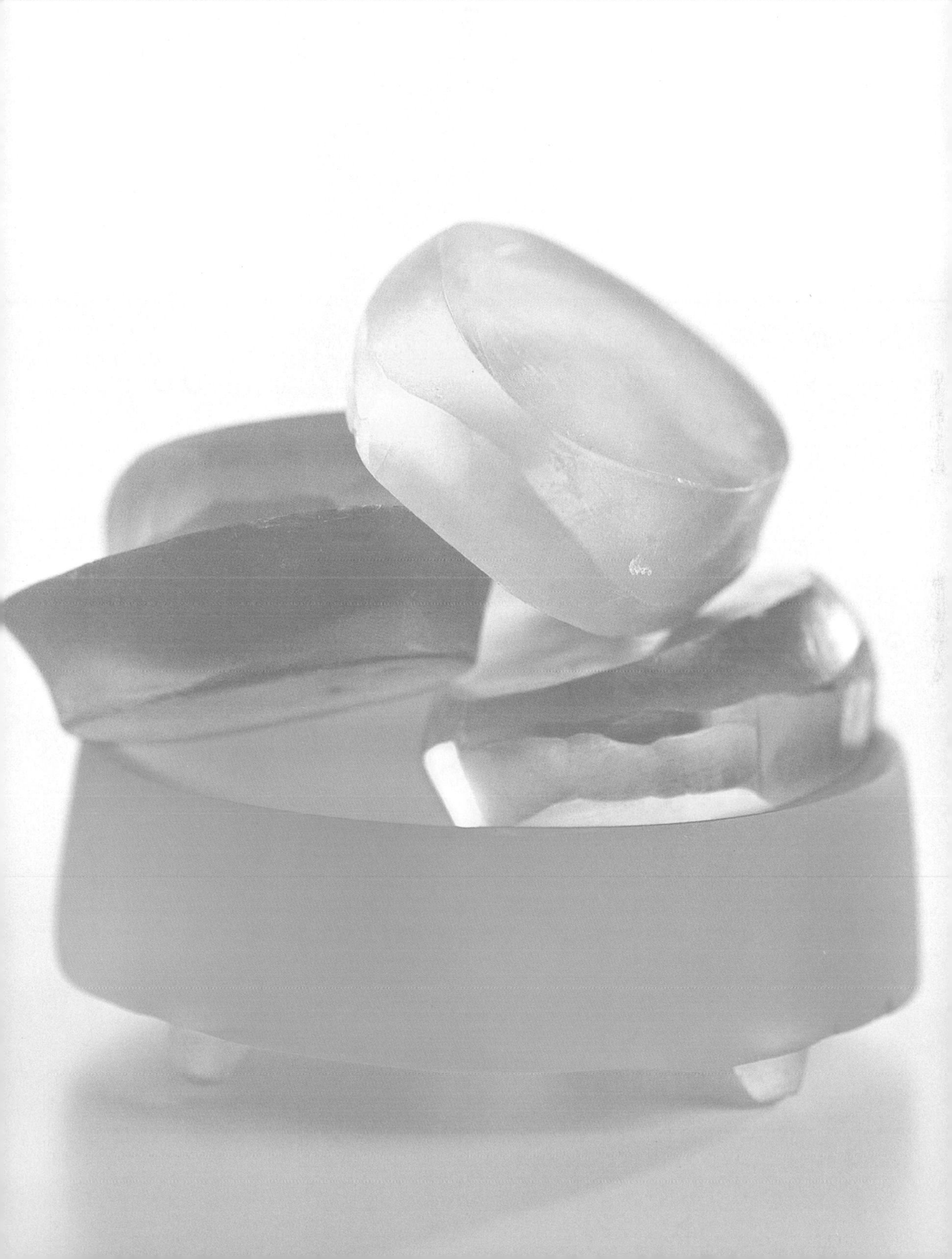

marble mosaic

This is made from the **assortment** of leftovers of different colors and textures that you will build up as you try out different recipes. The soap has a **sweet**, **floral**, earthy, yet **delicate** scent.

yield: 4 soaps
ingredients
2¾ cups/400 g grated block glycerin or glycerin soap pellets
¾ cup/110 g leftover glycerin soap
35 drops ylang ylang essential oil
8 drops vanilla absolute
6 drops vetiver essential oil
15 drops ho leaf essential oil

preparation

Following the instructions on page 14, fill the bottom half of a double boiler half-full with water and heat to a simmer. Place the grated glycerin or glycerin pellets in the top half of the double boiler to melt. Grease a rectangular mold.

Cut the leftover soap into small cubes, taking care to choose pieces with as much color and texture difference as possible. Sprinkle the soap cubes into the mold. When the soap pellets have melted, take the double boiler off the stove and add the essential oils. Stir well and pour the mixture into the mold, on top of the soap cubes. Leave for one-and-a-half hours in a warm place to set. Turn out of the mold, and divide into four blocks (see page 15). Store in a cool, dark place if not using immediately.

soap balls

18th-century wash balls

Adapted from an old recipe, these soaps can be used in the bathroom or kitchen. The **lavender** flowers add a wonderful, coarse texture with a **speckled**-egg effect. The scent is **herbal**, lively, balsamic, and refreshing.

yield: 6 to 8 soaps
ingredients
1–2 tbsp/15–30 ml dried lavender flowers
5¼ cups/400 g soap flakes
1 tbsp/15 ml laundry starch
2 tbsp/30 ml orris root powder
12 drops lavender essential oil
2 drops lemon essential oil
3 drops clary sage essential oil
4 drops FCF bergamot essential oil
3 drops benzoin liquid resin
1¼–2 cups/300–425 ml rosewater hydrolat

preparation

With a food processor or using a mortar and pestle, grind the lavender flowers to a powder. Place the soap flakes in a mortar or bowl and add the laundry starch, ground lavender flowers, and orris root powder. Mix together with a fork. Add the essential oils and mix thoroughly. Pour the rosewater into a microwavable container and microwave on low, or pour into a saucepan and heat on the stove until hot.

Add the rosewater, a little at a time, to the dry ingredients, grinding with the pestle. As more rosewater is added, the mixture will start to turn sticky and congeal. You may need to use a stainless-steel spoon to gather the pastelike mixture from the sides of the mortar. Continue until the paste resembles putty. Wash your hands.

Pour a little sunflower oil into your palm and lubricate both hands. With a spoon, scoop up a lump of paste about the size of a small apple and roll it in your palm until it forms a ball. Continue to form six to eight balls.

finishing touches

To achieve a smooth finish, add a little more oil to your palms and roll the balls until an even, outer shell is achieved. Place on waxed paper in a dark cupboard for three weeks until hard. This soap will keep for up to six months if stored in a cool place.

south sea island

These soap balls use monoi de Tahiti, a scent made from gardenia flowers macerated in semi-waxed **coconut** oil. The addition of **magnolia** absolute, nutmeg, and honey makes an almost edible concoction that is both **exotic** and spicy.

yield: 3 soaps

ingredients

1 cup/110 g monoi soap pellets
1½ cups/110 g soap flakes or 1 cup/110g grated cream soap
1 tbsp/15 ml honey
1 tbsp/15 ml glycerin
1 tsp/5 ml nutmeg essential oil
2 drops magnolia absolute
1 tsp/5 ml freshly grated nutmeg
1 tbsp/15 ml monoi de Tahiti

preparation

Following the instructions on page 15, fill the bottom half of a double boiler half-full with water and heat to a simmer. Place the monoi soap pellets, soap flakes, honey (heated if necessary to make it liquid), and glycerin in the pan. Turn the heat down low and let the ingredients melt slowly. The soap will take on the appearance of pastry dough.

As soon as everything has mixed together, remove from the heat. Let the mixture cool slightly, then add the essential oils, magnolia absolute, and freshly grated nutmeg and stir. Transfer the soap paste to a hard surface and work it with your hands, squeezing it through your fingers until it feels slightly elastic. Divide the mixture into three pieces, roll each one into a ball, and set aside.

finishing touches

Melt a little monoi de Tahiti in a small saucepan on the stove, or in a microwave on defrost setting. Apply a drop of monoi oil to your washed hands to lubricate them. Rub the oil over the surface of each soap ball form even, round shapes. Place in waxed paper and store in a dark, cool place for 48 hours before use. On a warm day the balls may exude a little oil. Wipe away any excess and place in a cool environment.

the moon's a balloon

These soap balls have colorful swirls of **purple** and peach, with a **marbled** effect. The scent is **fresh**, sweet, citrus, and soft, woody, with dry grass undertones.

yield: 3 soaps
ingredients
3 cups/225 g soap flakes
1 tbsp/15 ml orris root powder
1½ tsp/7.5 ml laundry starch
10 drops FCF bergamot essential oil
12 drops rose otto essential oil
11 drops atlas cedarwood essential oil
8 drops geranium essential oil
10 drops palmarosa essential oil
11 drops neroli bigarade essential oil
10 tbsp/150 ml bottled water
2 chamomile tea bags
5 tsp/25 ml red base color (see p.17)

preparation

Using a food processor or mortar and pestle, grind the soap flakes until they form a gritty powder. Place in a mixing bowl and add the orris root powder, laundry starch, and essential oils. Stir thoroughly with a fork until the oils are evenly distributed. Pour the water into a microwavable container and add the chamomile tea bags. Microwave on high for two minutes, or heat the water and chamomile tea bags in a small saucepan on the stove. Squeeze the tea bags in the water and discard the bags.

Measure out 6 tbsp/90 ml of the chamomile water and pour into the dry ingredients in the mixing bowl. Mix thoroughly with a fork and then, with freshly washed hands, knead the mixture. When the mixture looks and feels like pastry dough, pour in the red base color and mix the dye into the dough with your fingers to create a marbled effect.

Divide the soap into three sections and roll each piece into a round ball. Place a little sunflower oil in the palms of your hands and smooth the outer surface of each ball, pressing in any lumps or irregularities until you have an even finish.

finishing touches

Place on waxed paper for two to three days in a warm, airy place until hard. The longer you let the soaps dry, the harder they become.

forest fresh

The herbal aroma of **rosemary** and pine oil form this invigorating blend. The scent is intense, **lively**, balsamic, **minty**, and woody.

yield: 3 soaps

ingredients

1 tbsp/15 ml pumpkin seeds

3 cups/225 g soap flakes

1½ tsp/7.5 ml orris root powder

1½ tsp/7.5 ml laundry starch

1 tbsp/15 ml green base color (see p.17)

1 tsp/5 ml green clay

1 tsp/5 ml dried calendula flowers

1 tsp/5 ml wood betony

26 drops distilled lime essential oil

5 drops pine needle essential oil

10 drops fir needle essential oil

7 drops rosemary essential oil

20 drops field mint/ cornmint essential oil

10 drops atlas cedarwood essential oil

6 tbsp/90 ml bottled water

preparation

Grind the pumpkin seeds in a food processor or with a mortar and pestle. Put into a mixing bowl. Grind the soap flakes to a gritty powder and add to the bowl together with the orris root powder and laundry starch. Pour the green base color into the bowl. Stir well with a fork and add the green clay. Add the calendula flowers, wood betony, and the essential oils. Heat the water in a microwave or on the stove. Pour into the bowl and stir well. With clean hands, knead the mixture until it looks like pastry dough. Divide into three sections and roll each piece into a ball. Add a small amount of sunflower oil to the palms of your hands and continue to roll each ball, smoothing the surface.

finishing touches

Place on waxed paper in a warm, ventilated room. The soaps will be ready to use in a few days.

chocolate mint rolls

These smell **delicious**, almost good enough to eat. Real **chocolate** gives this soap a **creamy** soft, brown color, while the **aromatic** cardomom and cool, refreshing mint add to the sweet and **spicy** scent.

yield: 3 soaps

ingredients

3 cups/225 g soap flakes
1 tbsp/15 ml organic dark chocolate powder
5 tsp/25 ml hazelnut oil
1½ tsp/7.5 ml laundry starch
20 drops field mint/cornmint essential oil
15 drops cardomom essential oil
3 drops vanilla absolute
5 tbsp/75 ml bottled water

preparation

Grind the soap flakes to a gritty powder in a food processor or using a mortar and pestle, then place in a mixing bowl. Add the chocolate powder, hazelnut oil, and laundry starch to the mixing bowl. Stir thoroughly with a fork, making sure that all the ingredients are well incorporated. Add the essential oils and absolute and stir well again. Pour the water into a microwavable container and microwave for one to two minutes on high, alternatively heat the water in a small saucepan on top of the stove. Pour into the mixing bowl, and mix all the ingredients together with a fork or spoon.

When well blended, knead the mixture with clean hands until it resembles a pliable dough. Separate into three pieces and roll each one into a ball. Put a little sunflower oil in the palms of your hands, and smooth out any irregularities in the balls, so that the surface is even and smooth.

finishing touches

Place on waxed paper and put in a warm, airy space to dry for two to three days. The soap balls are then ready for use but will benefit from longer storage.

sharp shooter

This is a **tangy** soap with a buttery **lemon** color, made from an array of **citrus** oils, including may chang and petit-grain mandarin. In contrast to its smooth texture, this soap's scent is bright, sweet, sharp, and lemony, with a **floral** note.

yield: 3 soaps

ingredients

3 cups/225 g soap flakes

1½ tsp/7.5 ml orris root powder

1½ tsp/7.5 ml laundry starch

5 tsp/25 ml orange base color (see p.17)

20 drops sweet orange essential oil

10 drops mandarin essential oil

20 drops lemon essential oil

10 drops petitgrain mandarin essential oil

10 drops may chang essential oil

5 tbsp/75 ml bottled water

preparation

Grind the soap flakes to a gritty powder in a food processor or using a mortar and pestle, and then place in a mixing bowl. Add the orris root powder and laundry starch to the mixture. Stir together with a fork. Add the orange base color and stir well. Add the essential oils and stir again, making sure that everything is distributed evenly. Heat the water in a microwave for one to two minutes on high, or alternatively, heat in a small saucepan on top of the stove. Pour over the soap mixture. With a fork or spoon, stir thoroughly, then, with clean hands, knead the mixture until it looks like pastry dough.

Divide the mixture into three sections, and roll each one into a ball. Add a little sunflower oil to your palms and roll each ball again, pressing out any irregularities and creating a smooth, round finish.

finishing touches

Place on waxed paper in a warm, airy place. The soap balls will be ready to use in a couple of days, but if possible leave to harden for longer.

casbah

The color from the **mandarin** base, derived from mace, turns these soap balls a bright, sassy **orange**. You can vary the color by adding a mix of the spices alkanet root and turmeric. The scent is fresh, sweet, floral, citrus, **spicy**, and balsamic.

yield: 5 soaps
ingredients
3 cups/225 g soap flakes
1 tbsp/15 ml laundry starch
5 tbsp/75 ml bottled water
5 tsp/25 ml mandarin base color (see p.17)
5 drops patchouli essential oil
10 drops ylang ylang essential oil
14 drops FCF bergamot essential oil
14 drops mandarin essential oil
10 drops ginger essential oil
8 drops sandalwood essential oil
1 tbsp/15 ml wild rice

preparation

Grind the soap flakes in a food processor or using a mortar and pestle until they resemble a fine powder. Place in a mixing bowl with the laundry starch. Put the water into a microwavable container and heat in a microwave or in a saucepan on the stove until hot. Pour the mandarin base color into the ground soap and mix in thoroughly with a fork. Add the essential oils and the wild rice. Mix again thoroughly. Add the hot water to the soap mixture and mix well again.

With clean hands, knead the soap mixture until it looks like pastry dough. Divide into five sections and roll each piece into a ball. Wash your hands of any excess soap, and with a little sunflower oil in your palms, work each ball into an even shape, smoothing out any irregularities.

finishing touches

Place the soap balls on waxed paper in a warm, airy environment for a couple of days. Let dry in a cool, dry, dark cupboard for two weeks before use.

alchemy

The color of these soap balls magically changes from **cerise** pink through **purple** to a warm **brick-red**. The scent is rose, sweet-floral, herbal, fresh, balsamic, spicy, and **woody**.

yield: 5 soaps
ingredients
3 cups/225 g soap flakes
5 tsp/25 ml cranberry red base color (see p.17)
8 drops rose Maroc essential oil
6 drops ylang ylang essential oil
13 drops spike lavender essential oil
10 drops neroli bigarade essential oil
5 drops benzoin essential oil
8 drops myrtle essential oil
7 drops may chang essential oil
5 drops sandalwood essential oil
5 tbsp/75 ml bottled water

preparation

Grind the soap flakes to a powder in a food processor or using a mortar and pestle. Place in a mixing bowl. Pour the cranberry red base color into the ground soap. Mix well with a fork. Add the essential oils in sequence to the soap and base color, and stir in well. Heat the water in a microwave or saucepan until hot. Pour over the dried mixture and mix thoroughly. The base color will turn from a wonderful cerise pink to mauve as the hot water hits it.

Knead the mixture with your hands, and divide into five pieces. Roll into balls about the size of apricots, trying to form an even, round shape as you go.

finishing touches

Place the balls on waxed paper, and leave in a warm, airy space for a couple of days. Move to a cool, dry, dark cupboard for two weeks before use.

hips & roses

St John's wort oil has been used for centuries to **lift** the mind and body. Rosehip granules provide texture and turn this soap a light, peachy hue with a sweet scent of **roses**. Use rose geranium oil for a more **floral** aroma.

yield: 3 soaps
ingredients
1½ cups/110 g soap flakes
1 tbsp/15 ml rosehip granules
2½ tsp/12.5 ml St John's wort oil
8 drops rose otto essential oil
4 tbsp/60 ml bottled water

preparation

Grind the soap flakes in a food processor or using a mortar and pestle and place in a mixing bowl. Mix the rosehip granules into the ground soap flakes. Add the St John's wort oil, and mix together with a fork so that everything is well combined. Add the rose otto and mix again. Heat the water in a microwave for one to two minutes on high, or in a saucepan on the stove. Pour into the mixing bowl, and stir thoroughly with a fork until evenly dispersed.

With clean hands, knead the soap mixture until it resembles pastry dough. Divide into three pieces and roll each into a ball about the size of a small apple or apricot.

finishing touches

Place the soap balls on waxed paper in a warm, airy space to dry. They will be ready to use in one to two weeks.

quiet corner

This soap contains oils that have both a contemplative and an uplifting effect. Wood **betony** is added for texture and **calendula** oil for its soothing properties. The scent is earthy, floral, woody, and soft, with a **dry-grass** undertone.

yield: 5 soaps
ingredients
3 cups/225 g soap flakes
1 tbsp/15 ml laundry starch
1 tsp/5 ml wood betony
5 tsp/25 ml macerated calendula oil
1 drop vetiver essential oil
11 drops geranium bourbon essential oil
24 drops sandalwood essential oil
16 drops atlas cedarwood essential oil
10 drops palmarosa essential oil
5 tbsp/75 ml bottled water

preparation

Grind the soap flakes in a food processor or using a mortar and pestle, and place them in a mixing bowl with the laundry starch. Add the wood betony to the dried ingredients and mix with a fork. Add the essential oils in sequence, one at a time. Stir with the fork so that all the oils are evenly distributed in the soap. Heat the water in either a microwave or a saucepan until hot. Add the hot water to the soap mixture and mix in well. The soap will start to hold together.

With clean hands, knead the soap mixture until it looks like pastry dough. Divide into five pieces and work each piece into a smooth, round ball.

finishing touches

Place the soap balls on waxed paper and leave in an airy place to dry for one to two weeks, until ready for use.

purple haze

This soap is a beautiful, vivid purple shade. **Blackcurrant** and purple flower scents continue the theme. The scent is spicy, woody, **cassis**, herbal, camphorous, fresh floral, and haylike with **fruity**, tangy, and **lively** notes.

yield: 3 soaps
ingredients
1½ cups/110 g soap flakes
3 drops blackcurrant bud essential oil
5 drops spike lavender essential oil
6 drops clary sage essential oil
9 drops lemon essential oil
10 drops geranium bourbon essential oil
2½ tsp/12.5 ml cranberry red base color (see p.17)
4 tbsp/60 ml bottled water

preparation

Grind the soap flakes to a powder in a food processor or using a mortar and pestle, and place in a mixing bowl. Add the essential oils in sequence to the ground soap flakes. Stir well with a chopstick or fork. Add the base color and stir again, making sure that everything is well incorporated. Heat the water in either a microwave or a saucepan until hot. Pour over the soap flakes and stir again.

With clean hands, knead the mixture until it holds together like pastry dough. Divide into three pieces, and roll each one into a ball the size of an apricot or small apple.

finishing touches

Place the finished soap balls on waxed paper and leave in an airy place to dry fully. They can take from a few days to one to two weeks. They will then be ready to use.

orange tree

The oils for these soaps are extracted from the orange tree: neroli from the **blossom**, sweet orange from the **fruit**, hydrolat from the twigs, and petitgrain from leaves and twigs. The scent is **sweet**, fresh, bitter, warm, and intensely floral.

yield: 5 to 6 soaps
ingredients
3 cups/225 g soap flakes
5 tsp/25 ml shea butter
30 drops sweet orange essential oil
20 drops neroli bigarade essential oil
12 drops petitgrain bigarade essential oil
a good pinch of dried orange blossom
4 tbsp/60 ml boiled water or 5 tbsp/75 ml orange flower water or hydrolat

preparation

Grind the soap flakes in a food processor or using a mortar and pestle, and place in a mixing bowl. Heat the shea butter on low in a microwavable container in a microwave or in a saucepan on the stove until melted. Add the butter to the ground soap and stir well with a fork until evenly mixed in. Add the oils in sequence to the mixture. Stir well with the fork, making sure that all the oils are evenly distributed. Add a good pinch of dried orange blossom. Stir again. Pour the boiled water over the remainder of the dried orange blossom and let infuse for five to ten minutes, or substitute orange flower hydrolat, heated till hot. Add to the soap mixture. Stir with a spoon until it begins to hold together.

With clean hands, knead the soap mixture until it looks like pastry dough. Divide into five or six pieces and roll each one into a smooth, round ball.

finishing touches

Place the finished soap balls on waxed paper in an airy, warm space until dry. They will be ready to use in a week or two.

english idyll

The scent is evocative of verdant **gardens** filled with **daffodils** in spring and roses in summer. The soap has a rich, sweet, tenacious **rose** scent that is herbal, floral, and **green**.

yield: 3 soaps
ingredients
2 cups/225 g soap flakes
¾ cup/20 g oatmeal or ground oat flakes
1 tbsp/15 ml orris root powder
1 tsp/5 ml dried marigold petals
16 drops rose Maroc essential oil
7 drops narcissus absolute
½–1 cup/125–250 ml rosewater

preparation

Grind the dry ingredients, including the marigold petals, in a food processor or using a mortar and pestle. Place in a mixing bowl and add the essential oils and absolute. Place the rosewater in a microwave on low and heat until hot to the touch, or pour into a small saucepan and heat on the stove. Add the warm rosewater to the dry ingredients, a little at a time, and work it in well. Keep adding the rosewater until you achieve a stiff, pliable paste. Divide it into three pieces.

Wash your hands, and lubricate them with a little sunflower oil. Roll each piece of paste in turn between your hands, creating a smooth, rounded ball the size of a small apple or orange.

finishing touches

Place the soap balls on waxed paper in a warm, airy space for one to two weeks before use.

liquid soaps and gels

luscious lime

Lime, another citrus favorite, is used here with a **green** base for a **zingy**, colored liquid soap. Add the green base color to the soap and it turns a beautiful **yellow**, with just a hint of lime. The scent is **citrus** and sharp.

ingredients

2 cups/500 ml liquid soap base
2 tsp/10 ml green base color (see p.17)
1 tsp/5 ml and 9 drops distilled lime essential oil

preparation

Pour the liquid soap base into a container that has a spout. Add the green base color and stir. Add the distilled lime essential oil and stir well. Pour through a funnel into a glass or plastic bottle or pump dispenser. Cap, label, and use.

After a while, if you have added a base color, you may find that it separates if left standing. Just give the bottle a good shake to recombine the ingredients.

spice & minty shower gel

Palmarosa oil, derived from the aromatic tropical grass family that includes lemongrass, has **cooling** properties ideal for treating irritated skin. The scent is **sweet**, spicy, powerful, **warm**, minty, and grassy fresh.

ingredients

2 cups/500 ml shower gel base
6 drops cardomom essential oil
10 drops palmarosa essential oil
10 drops field mint/ cornmint essential oil
15 drops may chang essential oil
10 drops nutmeg essential oil

preparation

Pour the shower gel base into a container that has a spout. Add the essential oils, one by one. Stir well with a spoon or skewer. Pour through a funnel into a glass or plastic bottle or pump dispenser. Cap, label, and use.

immortelle shower gel

Helichrysum, also known as immortelle and everlasting flower, grows wild in the Mediterranean. It has a rich, **honeylike**, deep, **sharp**, clean, lively, **camphorous** scent with eucalyptus notes and tealike undertones.

ingredients

1 cup/250 ml shower gel base
10 drops helichrysum essential oil
16 drops lemon essentail oil
8 drops myrtle essential oil
3 drops Roman chamomile essential oil
5 drops black pepper essential oil

preparation

Pour the shower gel base into a container that has a spout and add the essential oils one at a time. Stir well with a spoon or skewer. Pour through a funnel into a glass or plastic bottle or pump dispenser. Cap, label, and use.

gingibar

Citrus and ginger essential oils, extracted from the root, complement the **vibrant** orange colors of this liquid soap. The scent is **sweet**, fresh, floral, delicate, **spicy**, woody, warm, soft, and **tropical**.

ingredients

1 cup/250 ml liquid soap base
1 tsp/5 ml orange base color (see p.17)
15 drops sweet orange essential oil
17 drops neroli bigarade essential oil
10 drops ginger essential oil
10 drops atlas cedarwood essential oil
10 drops ylang ylang essential oil

preparation

Pour the liquid soap base into a container that has a spout. Add the orange base color and stir. Add the essential oils to the liquid base. Stir well with a spoon or skewer. Pour the liquid soap carefully through a funnel into a glass or plastic bottle or pump dispenser. Cap, label, and use.

cedar's nest

Carrot **seed** pods fold in a circular pattern resembling a bird's nest. Carrot seed oil has a warm, **woody** aroma, which adds a distinctive note to this blend. The scent is sweet, warm, **fruity**, earthy, soft, citrus, **deep**, camphorous, and spicy.

ingredients

1 cup/250 ml shower gel base
5 drops carrot seed oil
8 drops atlas cedarwood essential oil
16 drops sweet orange essential oil
7 drops frankincense/ olibanum essential oil
8 drops bay essential oil
1 drop geranium essential oil

preparation

Pour the shower gel base into a container that has a spout. Add the essential oils one at a time. Stir well with a spoon or skewer. Carefully pour the liquid through a funnel into a glass or plastic bottle or pump dispenser. Cap, label, and use.

blithe spirit

This **vibrant**, colored liquid soap has a sharp **citrus** and **tangy** scent. A real "get up and go" to use in the shower after exercise or first thing in the morning, the scent is bright, **fresh**, lively, uplifting, **sweet**, and floral.

Ingredients

1 cup/250 ml liquid soap base
1 tsp/5 ml yellow base color (see p.17)
15 drops grapefruit essential oil
15 drops lemon essential oil
10 drops may chang essential oil
8 drops mimosa essential oil
8 drops frankincense/ olibanum essential oil
4 drops cardomom essential oil

preparation

Pour the liquid soap base into a container that has a spout. Add the yellow base color and stir thoroughly. The soap will become an intense yellow and more opaque. Add the essential oils one at a time. Stir well with a spoon or skewer. Pour the liquid soap carefully through a funnel into a glass or plastic bottle or pump dispenser. Cap, label, and use.

herbaceous border

This liquid soap is a truly vivid **strawberry** shade. The scented oils remind me of a garden **herbaceous** border. The aroma is **floral**, fresh, **sweet**, citrus, rich rose, **herbal**, camphorous, and spicy.

ingredients

1 cup/250 ml liquid soap base
1 tsp/5 ml cranberry red base color (see p.17)
20 drops geranium bourbon essential oil
20 drops FCF bergamot essential oil
5 drops rose Maroc essential oil
10 drops spike lavender essential oil
5 drops bay essential oil

preparation

Pour the liquid soap base into a container that has a spout. Stir in the cranberry base color. Add the essential oils one at a time. Stir well with a spoon or skewer. Pour carefully through a funnel into a glass or plastic bottle or pump dispenser. Cap, label, and use.

bath
products

moonlight milk bath

This creates a **soothing**, milky-colored bath, conjuring images of **Greek** goddesses bathing. The choice of **exotic** oils produces a **heady**, scent with **floral**, sweet, **warm**, and fruity notes.

ingredients

1¼ cups/300 ml milk bath base
3 drops tuberose absolute
4 drops Morroccan jasmine absolute
1 drop hyacinth absolute
2 drops French narcissus absolute
3 drops ylang ylang essential oil

preparation

Pour the milk bath base into a container that has a spout. Add the absolutes and essential oils one at a time and stir gently with a spoon or skewer until well incorporated. Pour through a funnel into a plastic or glass bottle. Cap, label, and use.

herb & forest shampoo

Lavender and rosemary oils are **rich** in nourishment for the scalp and hair. Lavender **soothes** while rosemary and **pine** are antiseptics that **stimulate** the circulation, adding a healthy luster to the hair.

ingredients

1¼ cups/300 ml shampoo base

10 drops lavender essential oil

6 drops pine needle essential oil

8 drops rosemary essential oil

preparation

Pour the shampoo base into a container that has a spout. Add the essential oils in order and stir well with a chopstick or skewer until fully blended. Pour through a funnel into a plastic bottle or pump dispenser. Cap, label, and use.

oat milk conditioner

This conditioner leaves hair **shiny**, soft, and manageable. Oat milk is good for the scalp while **mint** gives it a **refreshing** smell. The **scent** is minty, slightly **sweet**, and herbal with camphorous notes.

ingredients

¾ cup/175 ml white hair conditioner base

4 tbsp/60 ml oat plant milk

10 drops field mint/ cornmint essential oil

8 drops rosemary essential oil

4 drops lavender stoechas essential oil

preparation

Pour the hair conditioner base into a measuring cup and top with the oat plant milk until the total liquid measures just over 1 cup/250 ml. Add the essential oils in order and stir thoroughly. Pour the conditioner carefully through a funnel into a plastic bottle or pump dispenser. Cap, label, and use.

citrus bubble bath

The citrus oils impart a **sweet**, lively, and refreshing scent to this bright **yellow** bubble bath. Children will love the **sunshine** color and fresh aroma.

ingredients

1¼ cups/300 ml bubble bath base
5 drops yellow base color (see p.17)
25 drops sweet orange essential oil
25 drops lemon essential oil

preparation

Pour the bubble bath base into a container that has a spout. Add the yellow base color and stir well with a spoon or skewer. The liquid will start to look opaque and develop a color.

Add the essential oils, and stir well again with the skewer or spoon. Pour the bubble bath carefully through a funnel into a plastic or glass bottle. Cap, label, and use.

fruit & flowers bath

This is a truly **luxurious** bubble bath. Exquisitely scented **rose**, jasmine, and **neroli** oils are blended together with citrus and a touch of spice to create a rich, **creamy** indulgent bath.

ingredients

1¼ cups/300 ml bubble bath base
3 drops rose absolute
3 drops jasmine absolute
4 drops neroli bigarade essential oil
4 drops vanilla absolute
4 drops field mint/ cornmint essential oil
3 drops sweet orange essential oil
2 drops tangerine essential oil
2 drops coriander essential oil

preparation

Pour the bubble bath base into a container that has a spout. Carefully add the absolutes and essential oils one at a time. Stir well with a spoon or skewer and pour through a funnel into a plastic or glass bottle. Cap, label, and use.

sniffle snuffle blues bath

Following the aftereffects of a **cold**, this is a wonderful tonic for body and **soul**. The oils in this bubble bath have antiseptic qualities to help you breathe more easily. The addition of **lavender**, too, raises the spirits.

ingredients

2½ cups/600 ml bubble bath base

10 drops FCF bergamot essential oil

11 drops pine needle essential oil

13 drops tea tree essential oil

8 drops rosemary essential oil

8 drops field mint/ cornmint essential oil

5 drops eucalyptus essential oil

3 drops benzoin liquid resin

10 drops Roman chamomile essential oil

25 drops lavender true essential oil

18 drops lemon essential oil

preparation

Pour the bubble bath base into a container that has a spout. Add the essential oils and liquid resin. Stir well with a spoon or skewer. The bubble bath base will change in texture from being clear to opaque and become a little thicker in consistency. Pour through a funnel into a glass or plastic bottle. Cap, label, and use.

night flowers bath

Bathe in the **seductive** delights of this **oriental** perfumed bubble bath to emerge fragrant, pampered, and feeling **delicious**. The scent is heady, floral, creamy, **musky,** spicy, woody, fine, tangy, sweet, and rich.

ingredients

1 cup/250 ml bubble bath base
6 drops of FCF bergamot essential oil
8 drops lemon essential oil
4 drops tuberose absolute
5 drops rose otto essential oil
5 drops ylang ylang essential oil
2 drops cinnamon leaf essential oil
2 drops oakmoss resin
4 drops benzoin liquid resin
6 drops sandalwood essential oil
2 drops myrrh essential oil

1 drop ambrette seed absolute
6 drops mandarin essential oil
3 drops Moroccan jasmine absolute

preparation

Do not worry if you cannot obtain all of the many essential oils and absolutes used in this recipe. Even with a shorter selection, the end result will still smell wonderful.

Pour the bubble bath base into a container that has a spout. Add the essential oils and absolutes one at a time. Mix thoroughly with a spoon or skewer. The appearance of the bubble bath will change: it will become a little thicker in consistency and a lemony color. Pour carefully through a funnel into a plastic or glass bottle. Cap, label, and use.

soothing oat bath

Use this muslin bag of oats and soothing oils as a sponge or flannel to help **calm** your skin. Oats exude a **milky,** skin-softening fluid, while lavender and **chamomile** oils ease the spirit. Use once, then discard.

ingredients

⅔ cup/50 g rolled oats

2 tbsp/30 ml macerated calendula oil

6 drops true lavender essential oil

6 drops Roman or blue/German chamomile essential oil

additional materials

Cheesecloth (muslin)

Ribbon or string

preparation

Place the rolled oats in a mixing bowl. Mix the calendula oil and essential oils together, then pour over the rolled oats. Mix thoroughly with a spoon. Place a square of cheesecloth (muslin) flat on the table and turn out the rolled oat mixture into the middle of the square. Bring the edges of the material together and tie with ribbon or string to form a bag.

When taking a bath, soak the bag in the water and rub gently over your body. Discard after you have finished bathing.

bath frolic

When these tablets hit the bath, they make a wonderful **fizz** and release all their secrets – **exotic**, perfumed monoi de Tahiti, with **citrus**-scented distilled lime. Bicarbonate of soda is excellent for **calming** irritated skin.

yield: 4 bath tablets
ingredients
½ cup/110 g bicarbonate of soda
1 tbsp/15 ml cornstarch
3 tbsp/45 ml monoi de Tahiti
a good pinch of dried calendula flowers
2 tbsp/30 ml citric acid
40 drops distilled lime essential oil

preparation

Place the bicarbonate of soda and cornstarch in a mixing bowl. Either melt the monoi de Tahiti gently in a double boiler on the stove or place in a microwave in a microwavable container on defrost until liquid. Add the monoi de Tahiti to the dry ingredients, along with the dried flowers. Add the citric acid and lime oil, and stir with a spoon until everything is incorporated.

Spoon into small, shaped flexible plastic molds and press down firmly with the back of the spoon or the palm of your hand. Place in the freezer for 30 minutes or until solid. Turn out of the molds and put in a warm, dry place for one to two days to dry out. Store in a cool, dark place until needed – if there are young children in your family, this won't be long!

organic rose lip balm

This soothing lip lubricant has a soft, **peachy** rose tone. The rose and rosehip seed oils are especially good for regenerating skin. Alternatively, use **calendula** oil and **blackcurrant** bud, or field mint/cornmint oil.

yield: 5 small pots

ingredients

4 tbsp/60 ml rosehip seed or macerated calendula oil

¾ cup/150 ml sweet almond oil

15 drops red base color (see p.17)

¼ tsp/1.25 ml clear honey

¼ cup/25 g white beeswax pellets

5 × 40 iu vitamin E capsules

10 drops organic rose or blackcurrant bud or field mint/cornmint essential oil

preparation

Fill the bottom half of a double boiler half-full of water and heat to a simmer. Measure out the liquid ingredients, including the red base color and honey but not the essential oils, and pour into the top half of the boiler. Add the beeswax pellets to the mixture. Prick the vitamin E capsules with a sharp pin and squeeze the oil into the liquid warming on the stove.

As soon as the beeswax pellets have melted, stir with a spoon and remove from the heat. Add the essential oils and carefully pour into small ceramic pots. Let cool for about an hour. The melted liquid will turn opaque and harden. The lip balm will then be ready for use.

citrus herb deodorant

Here is a **natural** spray, which is antibacterial and **gentle**. The scent is fresh, **sweet**, herbal, floral, woody, delicate, lively, intense, and **refreshing**.

ingredients

4 tbsp/60 ml distilled witch hazel
1 tsp/5 ml dispersa
6 drops lavender essential oil
3 drops rosemary essential oil
3 drops ho leaf essential oil
2 drops FCF bergamot essential oil
3 drops lemon essential oil
3 drops distilled lime essential oil
4 drops neroli bigarade essential oil

preparation

Pour the distilled witch hazel into a container that has a spout. With a pipette or dropper, add the dispersa and the essential oils. Stir with a small spoon so that the oils begin to disperse in the witch hazel. The liquid will turn a white color. Pour through a funnel into a plastic bottle or dispenser with a spray cap, and label.

Before use, give the deodorant a shake to ensure that all the oils are redispersed. Make small batches at a time to ensure freshness.

fragrant linen spray

Spray this on your sheets for a relaxing, **peaceful** sleep. Calming bergamot has a **fresh**, fruity, floral aroma, and vetiver adds a rich, **earthy** fragrance. The scent is sweet, peppery, woody, green, and **creamy**.

ingredients

½ tsp/2.5 ml and 14 drops dispersa

6 drops mandarin essential oil

6 drops FCF bergamot essential oil

2 drops spike lavender essential oil

1 drop angelica seed essential oil

1 drop vanilla absolute

1 drop vetiver essential oil

4 tbsp/60 ml bottled water

preparation

Using a pipette or dropper, measure out the dispera into container with a spout. Add the essential oils and absolute, and stir with a spoon or skewer. Then add the water. Stir again. The liquid will start to look milky. Pour through a funnel into a glass or plastic bottle and screw on a spray cap. Label and use as required.

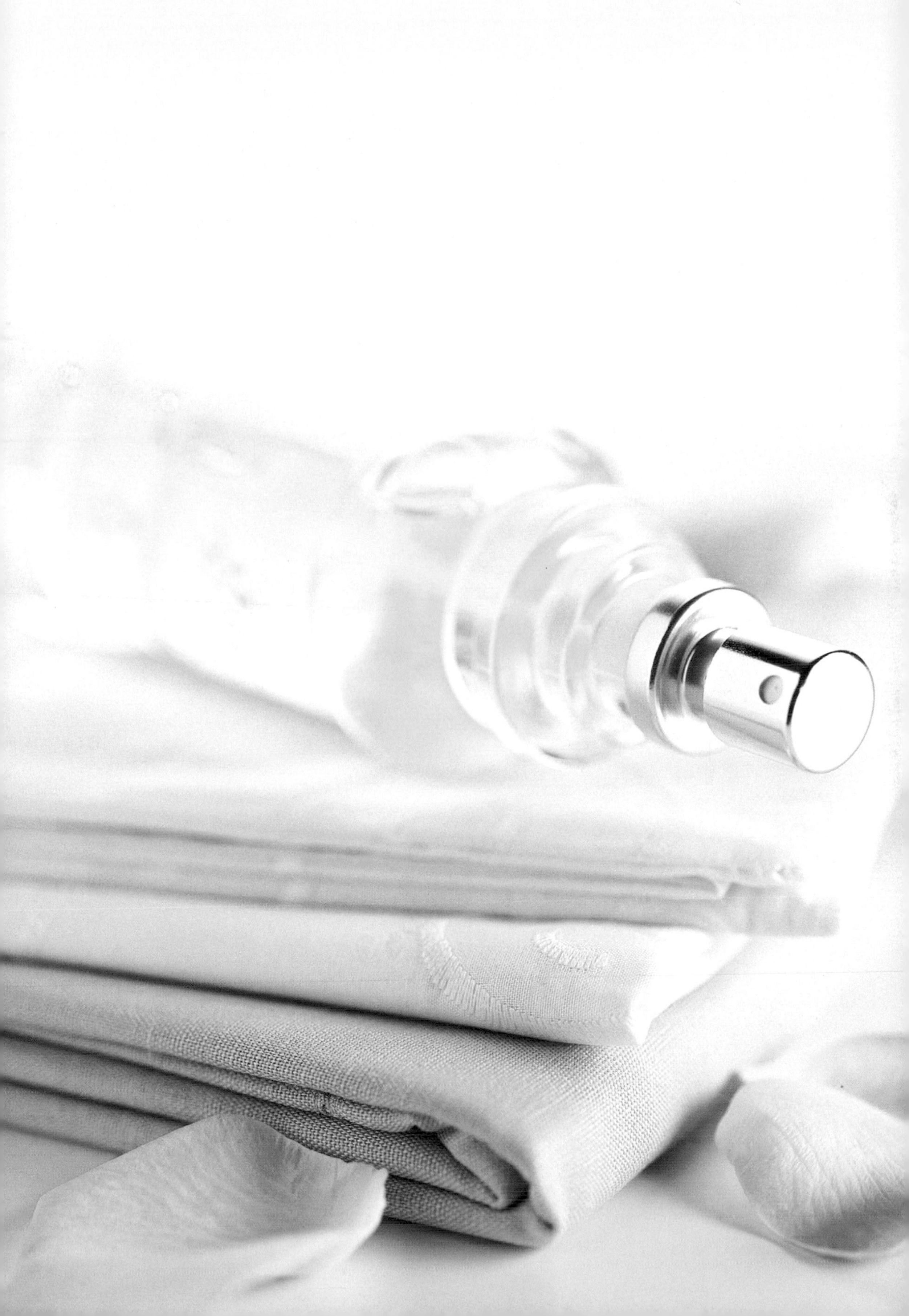

fantasy
collection

fantasy body mist

Cooling orange **blossom** water is combined with citrus oils to create a light and **invigorating** scented spray. Sweet orange oil has a warm, optimistic aroma while **vanilla** imparts a rich, creamy note.

ingredients

4 tbsp/60 ml orange blossom water or hydrolat
½ tsp/2.5 ml dispersa
1 drop vetiver essential oil
1 drop mimosa absolute
1 drop vanilla absolute
4 drops neroli bigarade essential oil
3 drops sweet orange essential oil
1 drop petitgrain mandarin essential oil
2 drops yellow mandarin essential oil

preparation

Pour the orange flower water into a container that has a spout and add the dispersa, essential oils, and absolutes. With a small hand whisk, beat thoroughly until all is incorporated. Pour through a funnel into a plastic or glass bottle with a spray dispenser. Cap, label, and use.

fantasy shower gel

The coolness of the **clear** gel contrasts with the sweet, warm scent of vanilla and **neroli**, a flower that is still a traditional ingredient in bridal bouquets. This gel has a floral, **fresh**, and citrus aroma.

ingredients

1 cup/250 ml shower gel base

4 drops vanilla absolute

3 drops vetiver essential oil

3 drops mimosa absolute

16 drops neroli bigarade essential oil

10 drops sweet orange essential oil

4 drops petitgrain mandarin essential oil

8 drops yellow mandarin essential oil

preparation

Pour the shower gel base into a container that has a spout. Add the absolutes and essential oils one at a time. Stir well with a spoon or skewer and then pour the shower gel through a funnel into a plastic bottle or pump dispenser. Cap, label, and use.

fantasy body lotion

After your bath, **pamper** yourself with this deliciously **fragrant** body lotion. Pure oat plant milk is **gentle** on the skin and, when added to a base cream, makes a light lotion fragranced with the sweet, **floral** "Fantasy" blend.

ingredients

5 tsp/25 ml bottled water
½ cup/125 ml moisturizing lotion base
½ cup/125 ml oat plant milk
2 drops daffodil yellow base color (see p.17)
2 drops vanilla absolute
8 drops neroli bigarade essential oil
6 drops sweet orange essential oil
2 drops petitgrain mandarin essential oil
4 drops mandarin essential oil
2 drops vetiver essential oil
2 drops mimosa absolute

preparation

Boil the water in a saucepan. As soon as it has boiled, remove from the heat, cover, and let cool.

Pour the moisturizing lotion base into a container that has a spout. Add the oat plant milk. With a chopstick or skewer, slowly stir the cream and plant milk together until they are well incorporated and fluid. Add the daffodil yellow base color and stir. Measure out the cooled spring water, add to the mixture, and stir carefully.

Add the essential oils and absolutes to the mixture one at a time. Stir well to incorporate the oils and lotion thoroughly. Pour carefully through a funnel into a glass or plastic bottle or pump dispenser. Cap, label, and use.

fantasy bubble bath

Start your evening with a bubble bath that will **revive** the spirits, uplift you, and **soothe** the day's cares away. The scent is sweet, **creamy**, intensely floral, bright, and rich with **fruity** undertones.

ingredients

1 cup/250 ml bubble bath base
½ tsp/2.5 ml yellow base color (see p.17)
3 drops vanilla absolute
12 drops neroli bigarade essential oil
9 drops sweet orange essential oil
3 drops petitgrain mandarin essential oil
6 drops yellow mandarin essential oil
3 drops vetiver essential oil
3 drops mimosa absolute

preparation

Pour the bubble bath base into a container that has a spout. Add the yellow base color, and stir with a spoon or skewer to mix the color. Add the absolutes and essential oils to the bubble bath base one at a time. Stir thoroughly so that everything is well blended. Pour carefully through a funnel into a glass or plastic bottle or pump dispenser. Cap, label, and use.

star fantasy

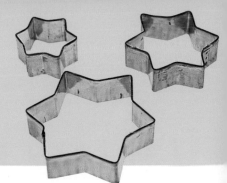

This soap is lovely, with the pale star **shining** gently in the middle of the round, **yellow** soap. The addition of **ylang** ylang essential oil imparts a **sweet** scent.

yield:

ingredients

1¼ cups/175 g grated block glycerin or glycerin soap pellets

5 drops daffodil yellow base color (see p.17)

8 drops vanilla absolute

32 drops neroli essential oil

24 drops sweet orange essential oil

8 drops petitgrain mandarin essential oil

16 drops yellow mandarin essential oil

8 drops vetiver essential oil

8 drops mimosa absolute

star: 1 cup/110 g grated block glycerin or glycerin soap pellets

12 drops ylang ylang essential oil

preparation

Following the instructions on page 14, fill the bottom half of a double boiler half-full of water and heat to a simmer. Place the grated glycerin or soap pellets for the main bar in the top half of the boiler to melt. Add the yellow base color to the melting soap mixture and stir. Grease a rectangular mold. As soon as the glycerin has melted, remove from the heat and add the absolutes and essential oils. Stir well. Pour carefully into the mold and let set. When firm, turn out of the mold.

Cut out two circles with a round cookie cutter, leaving the outer "frame" intact. Then, using a star-shaped cookie cutter, press out stars from the middle of each circle. You will now have an empty star in the middle of the circular soap. Place the circular soaps back in the soap frames, and put the entire soaps back into the rectangular mold.

finishing touches

To make the stars, melt the glyerin in the double boiler and add the ylang ylang oil once the soap has melted. Pour the melted soap very carefully into the empty stars in the middle of the circular soaps, trying to avoid any spillages, until the melted soap is level with the top of the main bar. Press the frame and the circles firmly to seal any gaps. Let set for a couple of hours. When firm, turn the circular soaps out of the mold. They are now ready to use.

fantasy body dust

The addition of the "Fantasy" blend of essential oils to the unscented **powder** adds a special touch and is worth the short wait before you can use it. The scent is creamy, floral, woody, **green**, sweet, **fresh**, and rich.

ingredients

¾ cup/75 g arrowroot
¾ cup/75 g cornstarch
2 tbsp/30 ml fine white clay
½ cup/125 ml dried orange flowers
1 drop vanilla absolute essential oil
4 drops neroli bigarade essential oil
3 drops sweet orange essential oil
1 drop petitgrain mandarin essential oil
2 drops yellow mandarin essential oil
1 drop vetiver essential oil

preparation

Measure out the dry ingredients and set aside in separate bowls. Line up the absolute and essential oils in sequence. Take the dropper top out of an empty aromatherapy bottle and measure the oils carefully into the bottle. As soon as you have finished, replace the dropper insert, ensuring that it is fitted firmly. Cap and set aside.

Grind the orange flowers to a powder in a food processor or using a mortar and pestle, and pass the powder through a fine sieve. Add to the arrowroot, cornstarch, and white clay. Add five drops of the blend from the aromatherapy bottle to the dry mixture. Mix thoroughly. You can use the balance of the blend for a bath.

Pass the whole mixture through a fine sieve, then put in a sealed container and store in a cool, dark place for one or two weeks to let the scent develop.

Suppliers

AUSTRALIA
- Purity Australia Pty. Ltd
Tel: 02 6685 6800
http://purity@nor.com.au

Organic essential oils and rare Australian oils.

- Select Botanicals
53 College Street
Gladesville
NSW 2111
Tel: 02 9817 0400
Fax: 02 9817 0500

email:
selectbotanicals@one.net.au
http://www.selectbotanicals.com.au

Essential oils, accessories, clays.

- Springfields Aromatherapy
Unit 2
2 Anella Avenue
Castle Hill
NSW 2154
Tel: 02 9894 9933
Fax: 02 9894 0199
email:
sales@springfieldsaroma.com

Essential oils, massage oils, oils for soap, base creams.

CANADA
- Ambrosia Essential Oil Apothecary
161 Lilac Street
Winnipeg, Manitoba R3M 2S1
Tel: 204 284 5014
Fax: 204 284 8401
e-mail: ambrosia@escape.ca
http://www.ambrosia.mb.ca

Essential oils, carrier oils, absolutes.

- Aquarius Aromatherapy & Soap
PO Box 3403
33191 First Avenue
Mission, BC V2V 4J5
Tel: 604 826 4199
Fax: 604 826 3322
email: adriana@aquariusaroma-soap.com
http://www.aquariusaroma-soap.com

Essential oils, soapmaking kits, molds, carrier oils, soap bases.

- The Aromatherapy Shoppe
At the Market Square
2109 Ottawa Street, Windsor
Ontario NBY 1R8
Tel: 519 253 6595
Fax: 519 966 3404
e-mail: aromatic@windsor.igs.net
http://www.windsor.igs.net

Essential oils, carrier oils, shampoos, skin creams.

- Essential Botanicals
Order desk: 1-888-327-1874
Fax: 519 824-8017
www.essentialbotanicals.com

Essential oils, flower waters.

- Plant Life
17 Lesley Street
Box 133
Toronto, Ontario M4M 3H9
Tel: 888 690-4820
Fax: 416 466 6458
email: maggiemann@plant-life.com
http://www.plant-life.com

Flower waters, body creams, aromatherapy accessories.

- Poya Natural Inc.
21-B Regan Road
Brampton
Ontario L7A 1C5
Tel 905 840-5459
Fax: 905 846-1784
Order desk:1-877-255-7692
e-mail: oils@poyanaturals.com
http://www.poyanaturals.com

Essential oils, bottles, shea butter, citric acid.

UK
- Fred Aldous Ltd
37 Lever Street
Manchester M1 1LW
Tel: 0161 236 2477
Fax: 0161 236 6075
email: aldous@binternet.com
http://www.fredaldous

Block glycerin, wax, rubber molds.

- Ascent Pure Fragrance
Natural Perfumery
Long Barn
Felindre
Brecon
Powys LD3 OTE
Tel/fax: 01497 847788
email:
morrisj@gonegardening.com
http://www.gonegardening.com

Soap recipe kits including essential oil blends and soap flakes or noodles, perfumes, after-shaves, scents, and soaps.

- G Baldwin & Co
173 Walworth Road
London SE17 1RW
Tel: 020 7703 5550
Fax: 020 7252 6264
email:sales@baldwins.co.uk
http://www.baldwins.co.uk

Essential oils, dried herbs, vegetable glycerin, dried flowers, base creams, oils, lotions.

- Butterbur & Sage
7 Tessa Road
Reading

Berkshire RG1 8HH
Tel: 0118 950 5100
Fax: 0118 957 6300
email:
butterburandsage@btinternet.com
http://www.butterburandsage.com

Soap pellets, essential oils,
absolutes, lotions, creams, soap
molds, soapmaking kits.

• Essentially Oils
8–10 Mount Farm
Junction Road
Churchill
Chipping Norton
Oxfordshire OX7 6NP
Tel: 01608 659544
Fax: 01608 659566
email: sales@essentiallyoils.com
http://www.essentiallyoils.com

Rare and exotic oils, absolutes,
monoi soap pellets, vegetable
soap flakes.

• Fragrant Earth Co Ltd
Orchard Court
Magdalene Street
Glastonbury
Somerset BA6 9EW
Tel: 01458 831216
Fax: 01458 831 361
email: all-enquiries@fragrant-
earth.com
http://www.fragrant-earth.com

Base products, shampoos,
essential oils, absolutes, plant
milks, vegetable oils, hydrolats.

• Hambledon Herbs
Court Farm
Milverton
Somerset TA4 1NF
Tel: 01823 401 104
Fax: 01823 401001
e-mail:
info@hambledonherbs.co.uk
http://www.hambledonherbs.co.uk

Organic herbs, spices, flowers,
petals, powders, flower waters,
flower essences.

• Nature's Treasures
Bridge Industrial Estate
New Portreath Road
Bridge, Near Redruth
Cornwall TR16 4QL
Tel: 01209 843881
Fax: 01209 843882
email:
naturestreasures@ndirect.co.uk
http://www.aromatherapy.ndirect
.co.uk

Soapmaking oils, caustic soda,
base products, essential oils,
hydrolats, specialty products

• Neal's Yard Remedies
15 Neal's Yard
Covent Garden
London WC2 9DP
Tel: 020 7379 7222
Fax: 020 7379 0705
email:
cservices@nealsyardremedies.com

Orris root powder, herbs, dried
flowers, cosmetic ingredients.

USA
• Amrita Aromatherapy
PO Box 278
Fairfield, IA 52556
Tel: 800 410 9651
Fax: 505 751 4571

• Aquarius Aromatherapy & Soap
PO Box 2971
Sumas, WA 98295-2971
(See Canadian entry for contact
details and website.)

• DCI Directory
Advanstar Communication
1 Park Avenue
New York, NY 10016
Tel: 212 951 6600
http:// www.advanstar.com

Trade journal listing materials
and suppliers for soapmakers.

• The Essence of Life
7106 NDCBU
Taos, NM 87571

Tel: 505 758-7941
email: info@newmex.com
http://www.taosnet.com/essence

Flower absolutes, oils.

• Essential Oil Company
1719 S.E. Umatilla St.
Portland, OR 97202
Tel: 800 729 5912
Fax: 503 872 8767
email: order@essentialoil.com
http://www.essentialoil.com

Essential oils, absolutes, molds,
infused oils, vegetable oils.

• Fragrant Earth
2000 2nd Ave Suite 206
Seattle, WA 98121
Tel: 800 260 7401
Fax: 206 374 9020
email: jade@theida.com
http://www.fragrantearth.com

Essential oils, absolutes,
shampoos, bath milk.

• Leila Castle Botanical
Fragrance
PO Box 302
Pt. Reyes Station
California, CA 94956
Tel: 415 663-1954
email: leilacastle@earthlink.net

• Leydet Oils
PO Box 2354
Fair Oaks, CA 95628
Tel: 916 965-7546
Fax: 916 962 3292
email: leydet@leydet.com
http://www.leydet.com

Essential oils.

• Sunfeather Handcrafted
Herbal Soap Company
1551 Hwy. 72
Potsdam, NY 13676
Tel: 206 525 4488

Soapmaking supplies, kits, oils.

index

acknowledgments

AUTHOR'S ACKNOWLEDGMENTS

My sincere and grateful thanks to: Chrissie Wildwood for her knowledge, friendship, encouragement, and advice, and also for the red base color recipe; Bernie Hephrun for talking and answering questions and sharing my delight in natural perfumery; Sandy Page who is always helpful and efficient to my aromatic orders; Mindy Green whose knowledge and trust I respect – thanks, girlfriend; Katie, Sarah, Simon, and Alison at Collins and Brown – what a team! Anne for keeping my house together; for my friends at Ffynnon Gynnon School for trying out my new recipes and giving me feedback, Little Martha (aged 4) for her loyalty to my new recipes; Dawn for coming to my rescue on the last push on the practicals; Caitriona for being there to help with Jemina and making me laugh; Catherine for giving me some golfing sanity … muchas gracias.

PUBLISHER'S ACKNOWLEDGMENTS

Many thanks to Ruth Baldwin, Loryn Birkholtz, Dawn Butcher, Claire Graham, Siân Irvine, and Alison Lee for all their help with this book.

BIBLIOGRAPHY

Arctander, Steffen, *Perfume and Flavor Materials of Natural Origin*, (Allured Publishing Corporation, 1994)

Cavitch, Susan Miller, *The Soapmaker's Companion*, (Storey Publishing, 1997)

Day, Ivan, *Perfumery with Herbs*, (Darton Longman & Todd Ltd with the Herb Society, 1979)

Dean, Jenny, *Wild Color: How to grow prepare and use natural plant dyes*, (Mitchell Beazley, 1999)

Keville, Kathy & Green, Mindy, *A Complete Guide to the Healing Art*, (Crossing Press, 1995)

Lawless, Julia, *The Illustrated Encyclopedia of Essential Oils*, (Element Books Ltd, 1995)

Maine, Sandy, *Soothing Soaps for Healthy Skin*, (Interweave Press Inc., 1997)

Stubbin, Carolyn, *Do It Yourself Pure Plant Skin Care*, (International Centre of Holistic Aromatherapy, 1999)

Watt, Martin, *Plant Aromatics Data and Reference Manual*, Researched and published by Martin Watt

Wildwood, Chrissie, *Encyclopedia of Aromatherapy*, (Bloomsbury, 1996)

CONVERSION CHARTS

Always use either metric or imperial measurements only in a recipe.
These conversions are approximate and have been rounded up or down.

weight		volume	
grams	oz	ml	fl oz
25 g	1 oz	20 ml	0.6 fl oz
50 g	2 oz	30 ml	1 fl oz
75 g	3 oz	60 ml	2 fl oz
110 g	4oz	75 ml	2.5 fl oz
175 g	6 oz	90 ml	3 fl oz
225 g	8 oz	150 ml	5fl oz (¼ pint)
275 g	10 oz	175 ml	6 fl oz
350 g	12 oz	250 ml	8 fl oz
400g	14 oz	300 ml	10 fl oz (½ pint)
500 g	1lb 1 oz	400 ml	13 fl oz
		450 ml	15 fl oz (¾ pint)
		600 ml	20 fl oz (1 pint)